$\mathcal{A}$nd these are the garments which they shall make, a breastplate, and an ephod, and a robe, and a broidered coat, a miter and a girdle: and they shall make holy garments for Aaron thy brother and his sons, that he may minister unto me in the priest's office.
And they shall take gold, and blue, and purple and scarlet and fine linen.
And thou shalt embroider the coat of fine linen, and thou shalt make the miter of fine linen, and thou shalt make the girdle of needlework. *Exodus chapter 28: verses 4, 5, 39*

Embroidery in the Church

Many fascinating examples of church embroidery exist today in old churches and museums around the world. A study of these pieces demonstrates that embroidery in the Christian church has always been strongly symbolical in both the colour and the design applied to the vestments, and the church furnishings.

Considering the period and the primitive conditions in which some of these older pieces of embroidery must have been worked, they show extremely high standards of craftsmanship in both technique and design.

Perhaps as a means of identifying themselves, the early Christians adopted existing pagan symbols, such as the circle, triangle, zigzag for water, and the fish, which eventually became the adopted symbol of the Christian.

It is interesting to note that the cross, on the other hand, is the most universally recognized symbol of Christianity, and is used in many different forms along with other early Christian symbols throughout church embroidery today.

A selection of early Christian symbols and crosses

Latin cross: the horizontal bar is placed high on the upright bar. It is also seen with three steps at the bottom (A).

Pagan sun wheel: an ancient symbol interpreted by the early Christians as the Greek initials XI, the monogram of Jesus Christ, within a circle (B).

Partriarchal cross: shaped as the latin cross but with two bars also placed above the center (C).

Fish and anchor: the fish represents Christ swimming through water to salvation and the anchor an emblem of hope (D).

Voided cross: this symbolizes Christ as the corner stone of the church (E).

Cross potent: this is one of the crosses used by the crusaders, and often seen in heraldry (F).

Y cross: this is an early symbol representing the expectant soul with arms outstretched (G).

Clavis: a cross surrounded with a circle, is seen extensively in Byzantine embroideries (H).

Circle: without beginning and end, the circle, or ring, is the symbol of God or Eternity.

Greek cross: has equal length bars, is a combination of fire and water and represents the creation.

Papal cross: also shaped as the latin cross with three bars in descending widths.

Cross crosslet: this is the Holy cross, also used in heraldry.

Symbolic use of color

It has been the tradition in the church to exercise certain rules concerning the use of color. These are governed by the seasons in the church calendar, and which the liturgical vestments and furnishings follow.

The colors are: white, red, green, purple and black, gold and silver.

White vestments are intended for festival days and seasons, and are the most richly decorated, traditionally with grapes and wheat ears.

Red vestments are worn by the priest on the day of Pentecost and the feasts of the Holy Martyrs, and on Holy Cross Day. These often have embroidered flowers worked in vivid colors.

Green vestments are used on ordinary Sundays and weekdays from the Monday after the first Sunday after Epiphany until Ash Wednesday, and from the Monday after the Day of Pentecost until Advent. The embroidery can be floral and colorful.

Purple vestments are worn during the season of Advent and Lent. During Lent the embroidery should not be flamboyant, but as a sign of penitence should be rather more austere.

Many contemporary designers have broken with convention, but before attempting to create new and original designs, it is well worth understanding something of the tradition behind the beautiful embroideries which we have inherited in the church today.

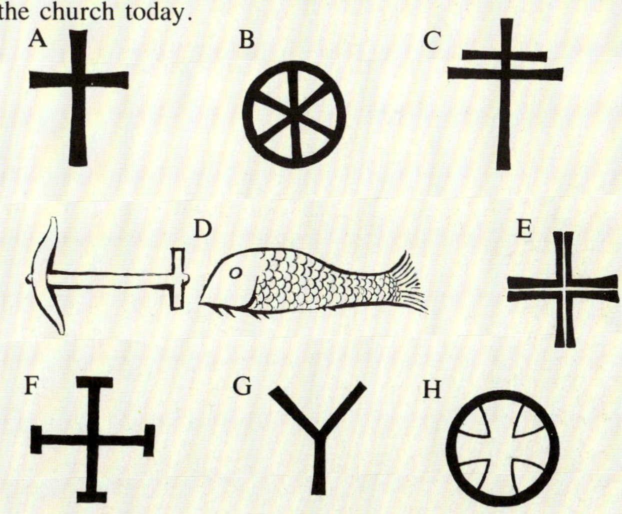

Early Christian symbols and crosses

Pulpit fall
The design on this pulpit fall admirably demonstrates the use of symbolism seen throughout church embroidery. The gold thread in the embroidery symbolizes the sun, light and learning; the circle, eternity; the three inter-locking circles (or triquetra), the Trinity; and the swords radiating from the circle form a monogram of the Greek letters XI (Jesus Christ).
It is richly worked with silver kid, smooth and check gold purls, and decorated with beads.

In addition to the embroidered liturgical vestments, there are other furnishings in the church which are also embroidered. These include the altar frontal, the dossal (an embroidered cloth hung at the back of the altar or at the sides of the chancel), the burse and chalice veil and the pulpit fall, which are used by the church officient to celebrate the different services of the church.

These vestments and altar furnishings usually follow the liturgical color of the season. For this reason, they are mostly designed as a set matching the color, fabric, the embroidered decoration, and the symbolic motifs of the particular season.

Since the pulpit is positioned so as to be seen by all the congregation in the church, it follows that it is an important focal point and therefore the embroidery on the fall should be boldly stated. The length of a pulpit fall may vary according to the height of the pulpit.

The altar is the most important symbol in the church and represents the Lord's Table. In history, the altar has almost always been draped or covered but not always with fabric. The styles and shapes of altar frontals vary enormously, from simple linen to heavily embroidered covers. Because of the importance of the altar, it is essential when designing the frontal to consider the entire church architecture, the scale of the interior, the color, and the strength of the applied decoration. The design should be bold enough to be seen clearly from a distance.

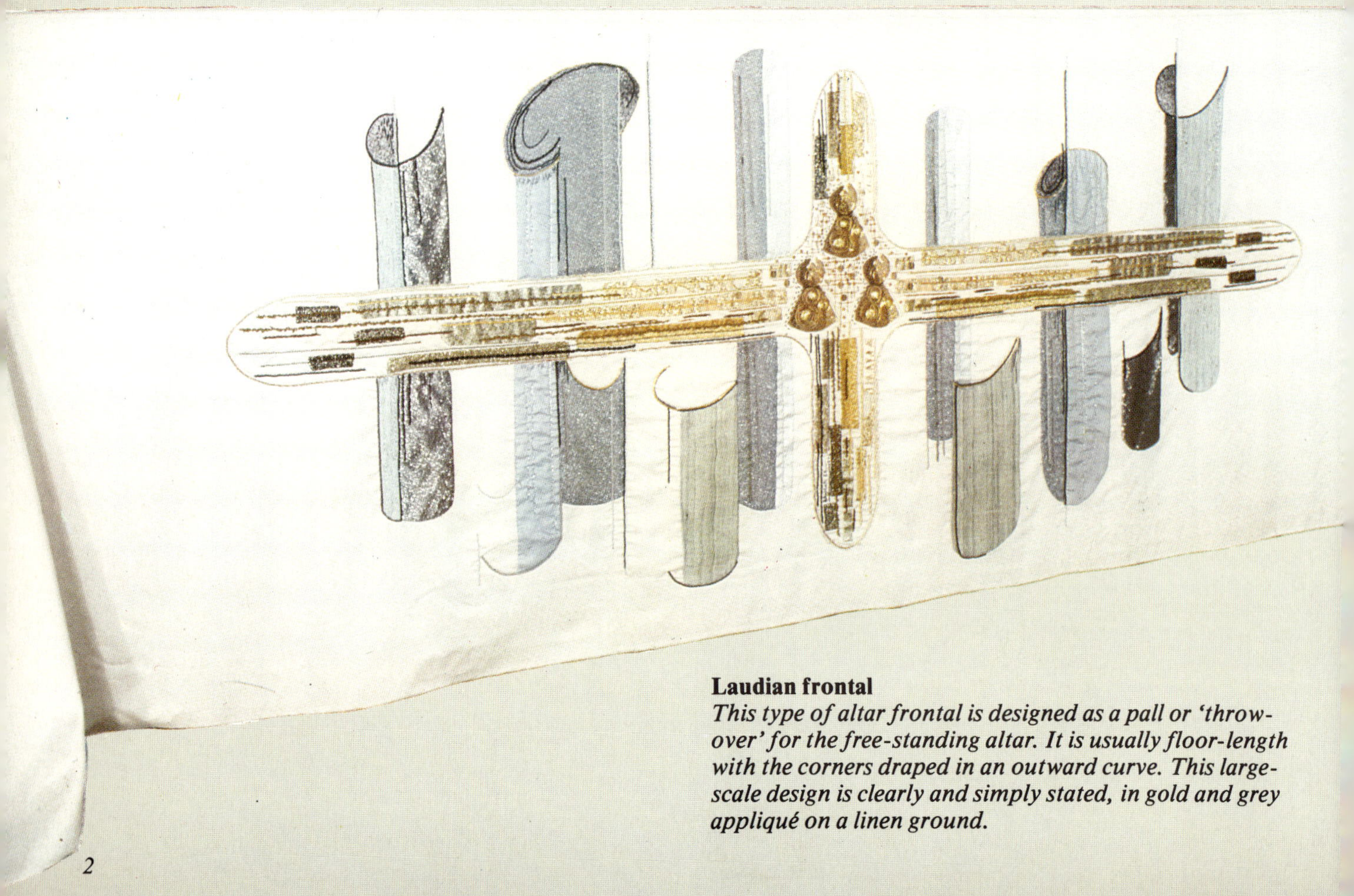

Laudian frontal
This type of altar frontal is designed as a pall or 'throw-over' for the free-standing altar. It is usually floor-length with the corners draped in an outward curve. This large-scale design is clearly and simply stated, in gold and grey appliqué on a linen ground.

The cope is the principal vestment worn for ceremonial occasions. It can be traced back through history to the Roman Paenula. Originally the cope was shaped like a chasuble with a cowl, or hood attached. It is semi-circular in shape and has richly embroidered orphreys, which when the cope is worn, fall together down the front as a single vertical trimming. The hood, which is attached to the back of the neck, is embroidered to match the orphreys. The cope is always fastened across the chest with a morse and decorated to match the other embroidery.

In designing the cope, it is important to choose fabric that will allow the front and back to hang flat, with deep folds at either side. In this way, the embroidery on the front and back will be clearly seen from a distance.

Pulpit fall
The classic simplicity of this design shows the three rings of the Trinity, with three doves representing the Holy Spirit, and worked in three colors only. The background has fabric patches under net which are decoratively machine-stitched in radiating circles.

Cope
This traditional-style cope is made from white and red damask fabric, bordered with Bodlean red orphreys which are richly embroidered with simple gold-colored crosses and spider webs, and edged with gold cord.

Morse
The detail of the morse, or clasp, shows an eagle motif made from gold kid. It is padded, applied to a damask ground and decorated with beads and bullion. The complete morse is edged with gold cord to match the orphreys.

Burse and chalice veil

Left *The burse shows the paschal lamb in the center of a latin cross, and is used in the church to celebrate Easter. The burse and the border of the chalice veil are finely worked on canvas with wool, gold and cotton threads, and decorated with pearls.*

Kneeler

Below *This canvaswork kneeler combines a simple clear-colored design with an interesting variety of stitches, which contrasts well with the church architecture.*

School banner

Right *This colorful banner, made as a group project, is based on the theme of 'Murder in the cathedral'. The main figures were worked separately in a variety of fabrics and threads which were padded and applied to a canvas background.*

The stole is a long, scarf-like garment worn around the neck over the cassock or alb as part of the set of liturgical vestments, and symbolizes the priest's authority. It is narrow in the middle and broader at the two ends, both of which are invariably embroidered. Wider stoles are often embroidered on both sides.

A single cross worked at the back of the neck is a fairly standard requirement, while any other embroidery worked on the ends may be quite varied. Conventionally worked stoles often have three crosses incorporated into the embroidery design, as the one shown below.

Banners and hangings can be taken into the church to celebrate particular feasts and seasons. They can be hung from on high, around columns and from their own supports attached to the pews. Many banners and hangings are specially made for Easter and Christmas and displayed during that particular season.

Although many embroidery techniques are suitable for banner making, machine embroidery and appliqué are widely used. They are excellent techniques for covering large areas where the design should be clearly and boldly stated.

Stole
The ends of the stole are decorated with Florentine patterns interestingly worked in a range of light-colored threads on a dark linen ground.

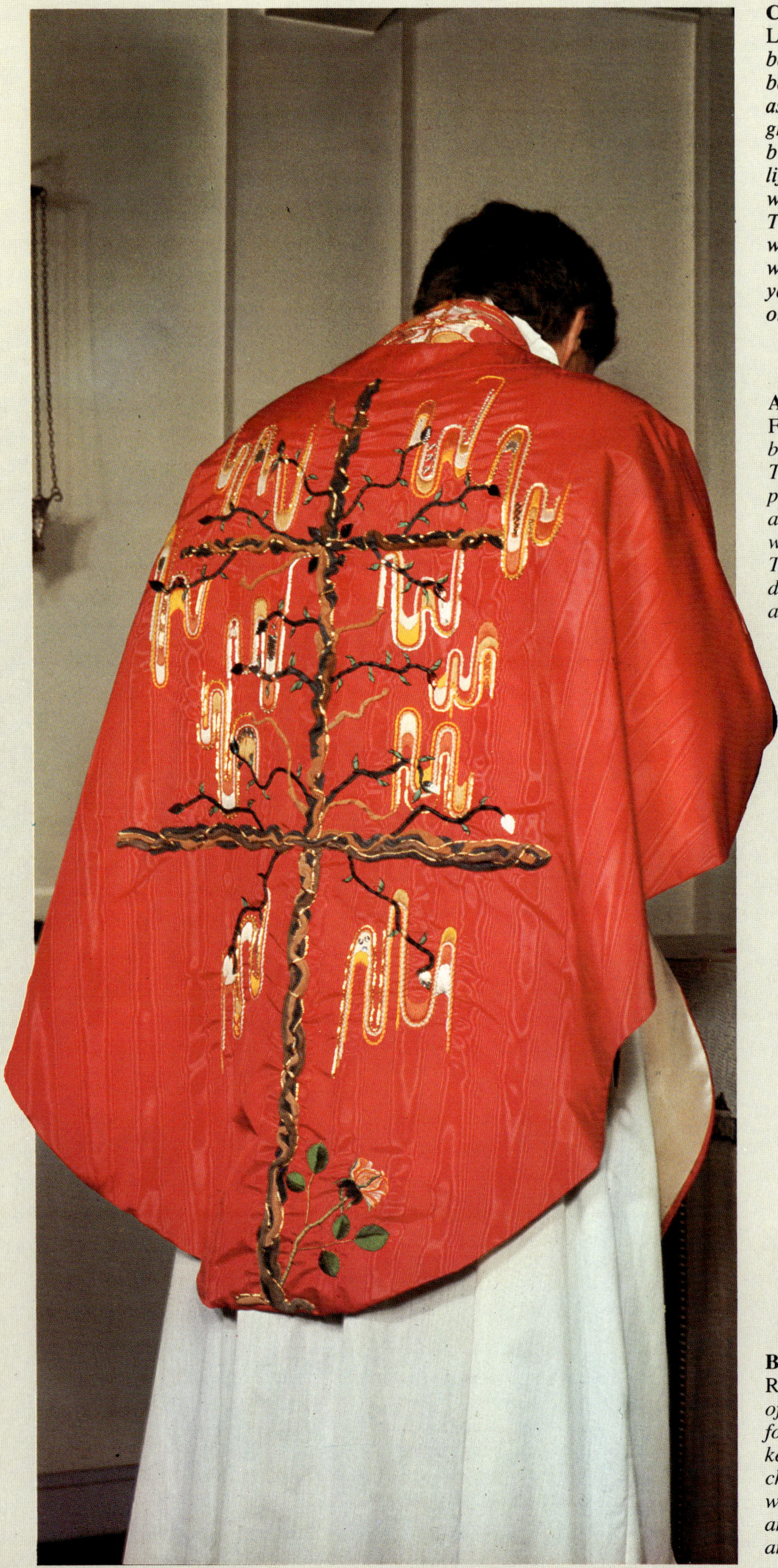

Chasuble
Left *The design embroidered on the back of* St. Catherine's chasuble *is based on the 'Burning bush' designed as a patriarchal cross. The rose growing from the bottom, and the buds on the branches, represent new life and resurrection, and thus, Christ, while thorns symbolize His passion. The gnarled bush effect is embroidered with twisted strips of leather entwined with gold, and the flames stitched in yellow and gold thread with silver kid, on a red silk moiré ground.*

Alms bags
Far right *This matching pair of alms bags are flat with a single pocket. They are worked on canvas, in practical colors, with a simple trellis and cross pattern, and embroidered with several decorative stitches. These include tent stitch, single and double cross stitch, Gobelin, mosaic and long armed cross stitch.*

Burse and chalice veil
Right *The phoenix is another symbol of resurrection which has been chosen for the St. Catherine's burse, in keeping with the veil motif and chasuble, opposite. The embroidery is worked in matching colored threads and fabrics using the same stitches and techniques.*

In the Christian church, the chasuble and alb are the official vestments for the celebration of the Holy Communion. The chasuble is the sleeveless garment which is rounded at the lower corners, and falls freely from the shoulders at the front and back. It can be decorated with embroidery, usually with a vertical band down the front and a large cross on the back. It is fastened at the front with two ribbons sewn inside at chest level.

The chasuble symbolizes the seamless garment placed on Christ after the scourging. It has, over time, been greatly modified from the earliest Paenula (a semi-circular garment joined down the front) to the thirteenth century garment with a pointed hemline, through the Roman shaped chasuble and the Gothic with its short hemline, to the shape of today which is longer and fuller.

In designing the garment, it is important to consider both the measurement of the wearer and that it has to be seen from a great distance.

The burse, which is stiffened and shaped like a book, holds the corporal when it is not in use. The corporal is made from linen and is usually embroidered with a border and small cross motif. The chalice veil which covers the chalice, is often made from fine linen and embroidered with a small cross integrated into the design.

SOLOMON IN ALL HIS GLORY
DID NOT SHINE LIKE THESE
CHURCH FLOWERS

Projects

In the following chapter, several canvaswork projects are given including church kneelers and a burse and chalice veil. They show a selection of designs worked in a range of colors, threads and fabrics, and a wide variety of stitches.

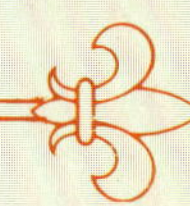

Compared with the sumptuous qualities of the silks, brocades and damasks, and the pure gold and silver threads that are required for much church embroidery, canvases and yarns are relatively plain. Perhaps, because canvaswork itself is a fairly straight forward technique and an equally satisfying pastime, it appeals to a great many embroiderers who might otherwise feel daunted by the expert stitching required for other types of church embroidery.

Working groups

Many churches have working groups within their congregation and it is through joining one of these groups, set up for making the church kneelers, that a great number of people become involved in embroidery for the church. Many embroiderers often go on to make other more elaborate pieces, finding the work both challenging and at the same time, immensely rewarding.

For the beginner, designing for kneelers can be quite an exciting challenge in itself. Certain governing factors have first to be considered; how the kneelers will look when they are seen either hanging in pews, or lying on the floor. The overall design should therefore be judged as a row of kneelers in the church environment and not always as a single kneeler seen out of context.

Types of kneelers

There are several different types of kneeler used in the church. The average size for the pew kneeler is about 9 in x $12\frac{1}{4}$ in x $2\frac{3}{4}$ in, or it may be larger and deeper, as in the kneelers given in the following pages.

Sometimes it is customary to hang the kneelers by rings attached to the back.

Sanctuary hassocks are usually much larger and deeper than the average kneeler, and unlike the standard type, would not be hung up because of the weight.

Communion rail kneelers depend largely on the architectural dimensions of the church and the relevant position of the altar for their size.

Kneeling pads are much flatter. They are made in a similar way to other kneelers but without the side gussets, and do require a ring for hanging.

The kneeler projects given in the chapter are designed to help both the beginner and the experienced needlecrafter in tackling not only a great variety of stitches, but to introduce new designs which will be suitable for different occasions.

Church furnishings

Canvaswork also makes an excellent fabric for other church furnishings, such as the burse and the borders on the chalice veil, also featured in this chapter, as well as the stole, alms bags, pew cushions, altar and sanctuary rugs.

Semi-circular plan of a cope showing hood and orphreys

Madonna kneeler

Work this attractive kneeler in diagonal tent stitch throughout using either the background color suggested or one of your own choice. The initial shown at the side of the window motif may also be substituted with an appropriate church emblem such as the cross, and stitched in a contrasting color.

Size

10 in x 15 in x 3 in

Materials

$23\frac{1}{2}$ in of $26\frac{3}{4}$ in–wide single canvas with 10 threads to 1 in
Anchor tapestry wool in the following amounts and colors: 4 skeins light blue 0508; 3 skeins beige 0899; 2 skeins each cream 0386, mid gold 0306, pale yellow 0305, grey blue 0147, brown 0424, black 0403; 1 skein each gold 0308, white 0402 and 60 skeins blue 0132 for background
10 in x 15 in x 3 in deep of compressed foam
10 in x 15 in of thin leather, or a suitable alternative such as vinyl or hessian, for the base
Slate frame with $26\frac{3}{4}$ in tapes
Size 16 tapestry needle
Three-sided leather needle
Wadding (optional) Linen thread

Stitches and techniques

For the following stitches and techniques, see pages 21, 22, 30, 31 and 32.
Beginning to stitch and fastening off
Diagonal tent stitch
Dressing a slate frame
Blocking the canvas
Lacing the back of the kneeler

Instructions

Using either a soft pencil or colored tacking thread, mark the center of the canvas both ways. Then, following the measurement diagram given opposite, mark the outline of the kneeler, measuring from the center outwards. Stretch the canvas in the frame, see page 30, or if you intend working the canvas in the hand, bind the raw edges with masking tape. This will prevent the canvas from fraying and the yarn from catching.

Embroidery

Following the color chart given opposite, begin with the madonna and work outwards from the middle. Complete the madonna motif and any additional initials or emblems at either side, before working the background and side sections.

Using double yarn in the needle, work diagonal tent stitch throughout, see page 22, except for outlining the madonna and window, where it will be necessary to work both horizontal and vertical tent stitches to fit. Embroider the second emblem by working in reverse from the center lines.

Complete the background and carefully trim any loose ends on the wrong side. Remove the embroidery from the frame without cutting the surrounding canvas. Block the canvas if necessary, by damp stretching and leaving to dry naturally, see page 31.

Making up

Cut out the kneeler allowing an extra $\frac{3}{4}$ in all round for seams. With right sides together, pin out the two side sections at each corner to form a box shape. Using strong thread, stitch the four corners. Trim corners and seams. Turn through to right side, finger pressing the seams flat. Insert the foam pad pushing well into the corners to make a firm, rectangular shape. If required, insert extra loose wadding to fill out the corners. Fold the turnings on the canvas under the base and crease the edges firmly. Either stitch the canvas turning to the foam using strong thread and herringbone stitch, or lace the opposite sides together, see page 32. Next, cover the base with leather to neaten. Using a fine needle and thread, hold the leather in place by stitching it to the canvas edge once in the middle of each side. Tie the thread and trim. Then, using a firm needle and strong thread, hem the leather in place. Remove holding threads to finish. Alternatively, for a hessian base, first cut the fabric to size allowing an extra $\frac{3}{4}$ in all round for seams. Then, fold turnings to wrong side and pin in place. With matching thread, hem all four sides to finish.

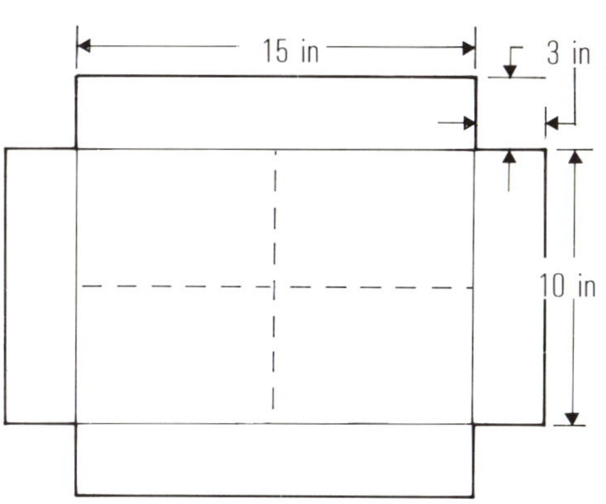

Measurement Diagram

1 square = one tent stitch

centre line

Color Key

▦	0508	▦	0424
▦	0899	■	0403
▦	0386	▦	0308
▦	0306	▦	0402
▦	0305		0132
▦	0147		

Contemporary cross kneeler

Embroider this cleverly designed kneeler in clear colors and diagonal tent stitch throughout. The design is an abstract arrangement of both the simple cross and the Holy cross formations. The sides of the kneeler are worked in tent stitch using the same background color.

Size

10 in x 15 in x 3 in

Materials

$23\frac{1}{2}$ in of $26\frac{3}{4}$ in-wide single canvas with 10 threads to 1 in
Anchor tapestry wool in the following amounts and colors: 10 skeins cream 0386; 8 skeins dark grey 0849; 6 skeins blue 0140; 4 skeins red 019 and 58 skeins light grey 0144 for the background.
10 in x 15 in x 3 in deep of compressed foam
30 in x $32\frac{1}{4}$ in of unbleached calico
$10\frac{3}{4}$ in x $15\frac{3}{4}$ in of holland or upholsterer's linen for the base
Slate frame with $26\frac{3}{4}$ in tapes
Size 18 tapestry needle
Synthetic wadding (optional)
Strong thread

Stitches and techniques

For the following stitches and techniques, see pages 21, 22, 30, 31 and 32.

Beginning to stitch and fastening off
Diagonal tent stitch
Horizontal tent stitch
Dressing a slate frame
Blocking the canvas
Covering the kneeler with calico.

Instructions

Mark the center of the canvas both ways using either a soft pencil or colored tacking threads. Then, following the measurement diagram given opposite, mark the outline of the kneeler carefully working outwards from the center. Mount the canvas into the frame, see page 30, or if you plan to work in the hand, either cover the raw edges with masking tape or turn in and stitch the edges. This will prevent the canvas from fraying and the yarn from catching.

Embroidery

Use double yarn in the needle throughout. Following the color chart given opposite and working diagonal tent stitch, see page 22, begin with the central cross. Continue working the design outwards from the middle using vertical tent stitch and horizontal tent stitch where appropriate. Embroider the stronger colors first leaving the cream and light grey until last. Outline the top of the kneeler with dark grey before working the side sections in light grey to complete the embroidery.

Remove the whole of the embroidered canvas from the frame and neaten any loose ends of yarn. If necessary, damp stretch the canvas, see page 31.

Making up

When completetly dry, cut out the kneeler allowing $\frac{3}{4}$ in all round for seams. With right sides together, pin the two side sections at each corner to form a box shape. With strong thread in the needle (carpet sharp) stab stitch the four corners. Trim across corners and seams. Turn through to right side and finger press seams open. To give extra support to the foam pad, it is sometimes advisable to cover it first with fabric, see page 32.

Insert the covered foam into the kneeler, adding extra wadding at the corners if necessary, to make a firm rectangular pad. Fold the turnings on the canvas under the base creasing the edges firmly. Stitch to calico using herringbone stitch.

Neaten the bottom of the kneeler with holland or upholsterer's linen: for leather, imitation leather or hessian, see Madonna Kneeler. Fold 1 in turnings to the wrong side neatly mitering the corners. Pin in place pulling the fabric straight and tight. Using matching strong thread, stitch neatly around each side.

Color Key

◼ 019		◻ 0386	
◼ 0140		◻ 0144	
◼ 0849			

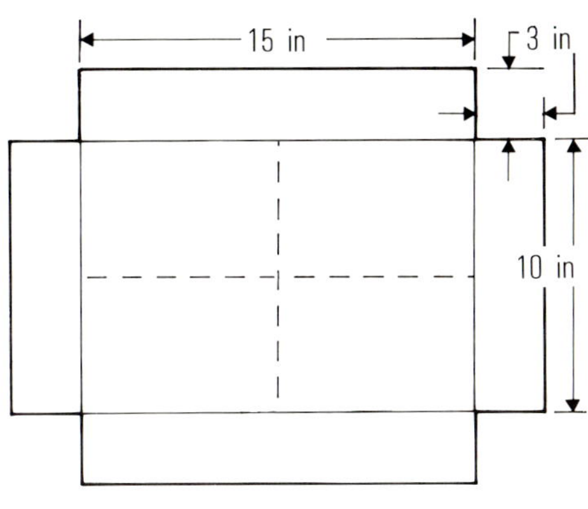

Measurement Diagram

1 square = 1 tent stitch

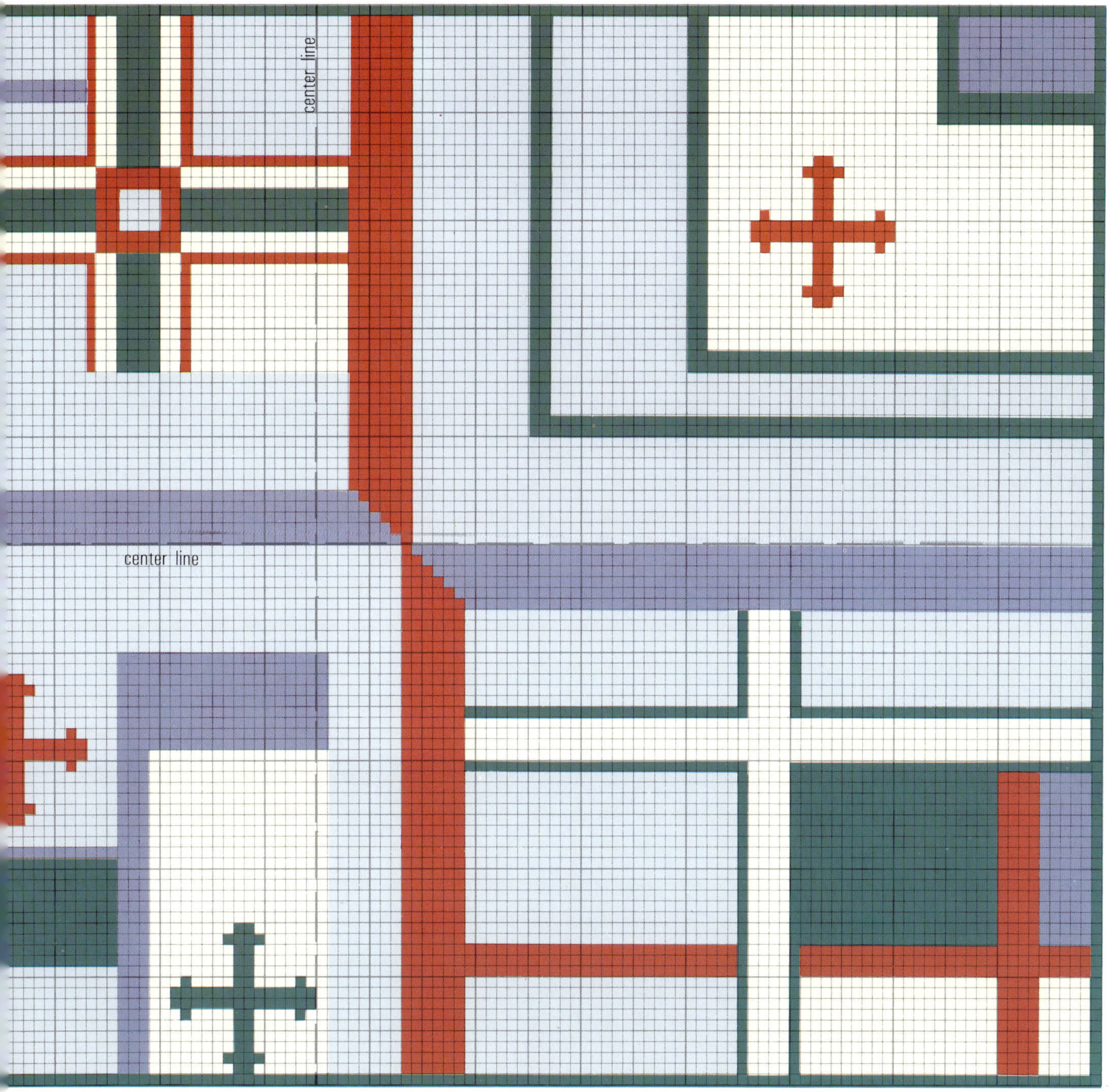

Burse and chalice veil

Work this beautiful burse and chalice veil in contrasting threads, decorated with lurex and pearls. The burse shows the paschal lamb centered on a latin cross with the initials IHS on the back. The border of the veil is embroidered with a simple cross in each corner in matching threads and pearls.

Size

Burse $9\frac{1}{2}$ in square
Veil $26\frac{1}{2}$ in square

Materials

$19\frac{3}{4}$ in of $26\frac{1}{2}$ in wide white single canvas with 18 threads to 1 in
Crewel yarn in the following amounts and colors: 9 skeins each Heraldic gold 1 and 4; 2 skeins each Heraldic gold 2, Elephant grey 3, and Brown grounding 4; 1 skein Brown olive 1 Anchor stranded embroidery thread in the following amounts and colors: 8 skeins dark blue 0143; 4 skeins cream 0386; 3 skeins pale blue 0120; 2 skeins fawn 0390; 1 skein white 0402 and oddments of scarlet 046 and brown 0375
Six skeins of untarnishable gold cord, Code B 129
$39\frac{1}{2}$ in of $29\frac{1}{2}$ in-wide fine white linen
White and dark blue sewing threads

Approximately 600 white pearls, $\frac{1}{8}$ in across
Slate frame with $26\frac{1}{2}$ in tapes
Size 20 tapestry needle
19 in x $19\frac{3}{4}$ in of stiff white mounting board
White poster color and fine paint brush
All purpose clear adhesive

Stitches and techniques

For the following stitches and techniques, see pages 22, 24, 25, 26, 27, 30 and 32.

Diagonal tent stitch
Cross stitch
Double cross stitch
Eye stitch
Counted satin stitch
Back stitch
Dressing a slate frame
Mounting fabric on cardboard
Stitching the spine to the burse

Instructions

Following the measurement and layout diagram, and with a soft pencil, outline all the pieces as shown. Enlarge the embroidery designs given opposite for the front and back of the burse, where one square equals $\frac{1}{2}$ in. Strengthen the outline with black felt tip. Place canvas over designs, and with outer lines matching, secure with adhesive tape or drawing pins. Using the fine brush and poster paint, lightly trace through the main outlines.
Stretch the canvas in to the frame, see page 30, with the burse designs and veil corners placed in the middle. Roll remaining canvas around roller, to be worked later.

Embroidery

The embroidery is worked throughout with double yarn in the needle.

Burse Front

Color Key

Anchor stranded embroidery thread

☐ 0402		■ 0143	
☐ 0386		■ 046	
☐ 0390		■ 0375	
☐ 0120			

Crewel yarn

- Heraldic gold 1
- Heraldic gold 2
- Heraldic gold 4
- Elephant grey 3
- Brown olive 1
- Brown grounding 4
- Gold cord

Stitch Key

A Tent stitch

B Tent stitch with pearls

C Tent stitch with random single cross stitch

D Random eyelets with tent stitch

E Tent stitch with random single eyelets and double cross stitch

F Tent stitch with random blocks of cross stitch

G Cross stitch (over one thread intersection)

H Back stitch

I Counted satin stitch with random diagonal stitch squares

J Eye stitch

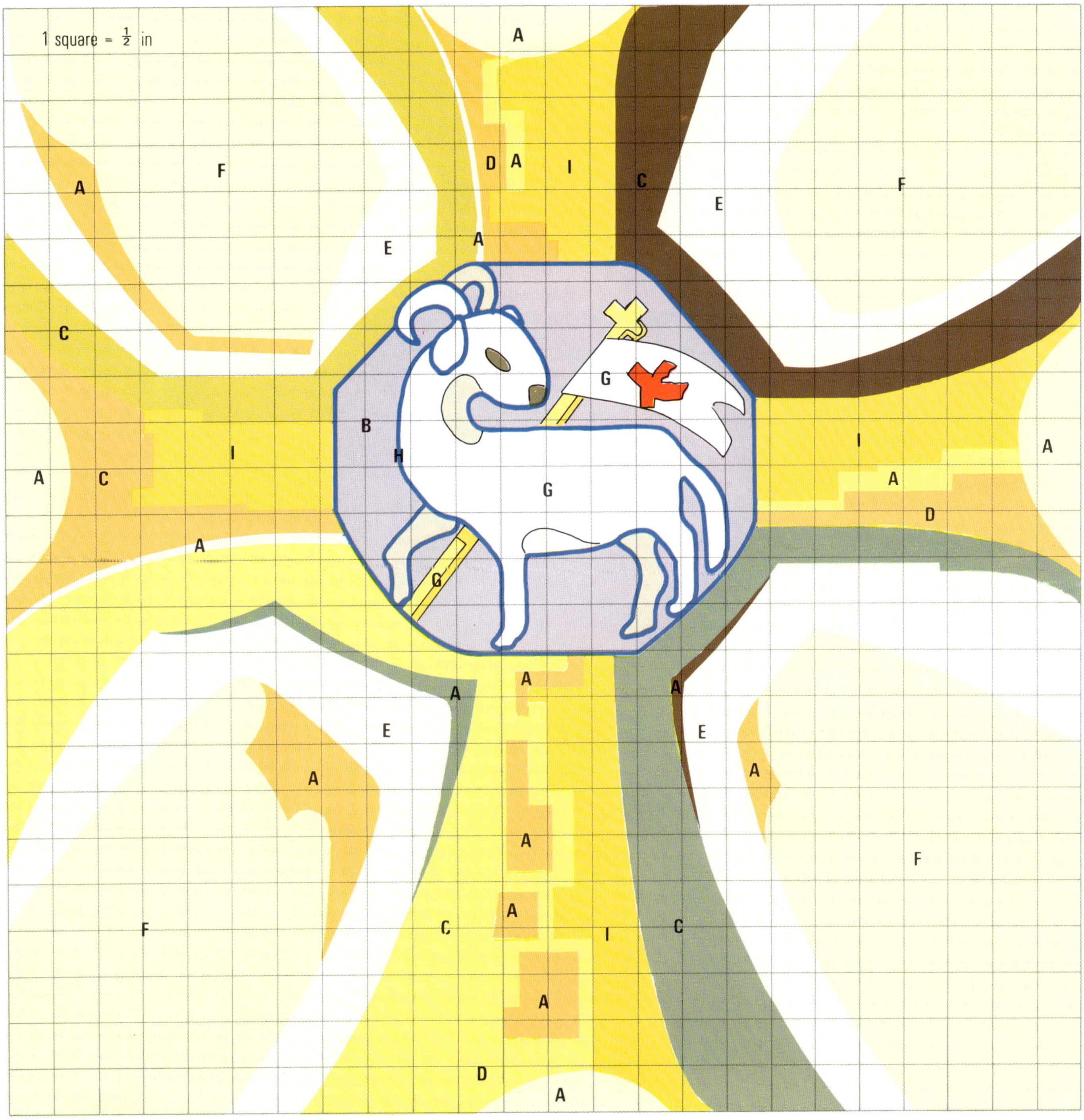

Burse front Following the color and stitch keys, begin the embroidery with the lamb and work outwards from the middle. Work the center of the large cross in counted satin stitch with random squares of diagonal stitches, bordered with tent stitch, as shown. On the opposite side, work the random eyelets of (D) first and then fill in the background with tent stitch. Then work (C), embroidering random cross stitches over two threads before filling the background with tent stitch. For (E), work eyelets over five threads and double cross stitch over two with tent stitch background. For (F), work random blocks of cross stitch over two threads (about five or six stitches) on a tent stitch background. Outline some of the

stitch background. Outline some of the crosses with gold thread.

Complete the embroidery, filling in the remaining areas with tent stitch in the appropriate colors. Outline the lamb with back stitch before adding the pearls to the background. Using matching sewing thread, place them in vertical rows at $\frac{1}{4}$ in intervals.

Burse back Following the color and stitch keys, begin the embroidery with the initials and work outwards from the middle. Complete the motif before embroidering the background (F), working as for the front in blocks of cross stitch, outlining some of the crosses with gold thread. Outline the initials with back stitch and apply the pearls at $\frac{1}{4}$ in intervals to complete the embroidery.

Spine Using the same yarn as for the background, work the $\frac{3}{4}$ in-wide spine in tent stitch. Place centrally on canvas allowing $\frac{1}{2}$ in turnings at each side.

Veil Following the color chart given, work the four corners, each measuring $1\frac{1}{2}$ in square, leaving $\frac{1}{2}$ in turnings all round. Adjust the canvas if necessary by rolling the finished embroidery around the top of the frame, ready to work the veil borders. Complete each section of border working the eyelets of (J) in gold thread, over five threads, and the second section in tent stitch. This completes the embroidery. Remove canvas from frame. Refer to cutting layout and cut out burse adding $1\frac{1}{4}$ in seam allowances. Cut out spine, veil borders and corners as instructed.

Making up

Cutting out From the cardboard, cut out four squares each measuring $9\frac{1}{2}$ in (two pieces for the outer cover and two for the lining of the burse), and one length $9\frac{1}{2}$ in x $\frac{3}{4}$ in for the spine. Press the linen to remove all creases. For the chalice veil, cut out one square measuring 28 in; this includes $\frac{1}{2}$ in turnings all round. For the burse lining, cut out two squares each measuring $11\frac{1}{2}$ in; this includes 1 in turnings all round. From the remaining linen, cut out one section measuring $1\frac{1}{2}$ in x $11\frac{3}{4}$ in for the spine.

Mounting the embroidery Mark the center of each piece of card both ways. (Sometimes it is better to have thinner

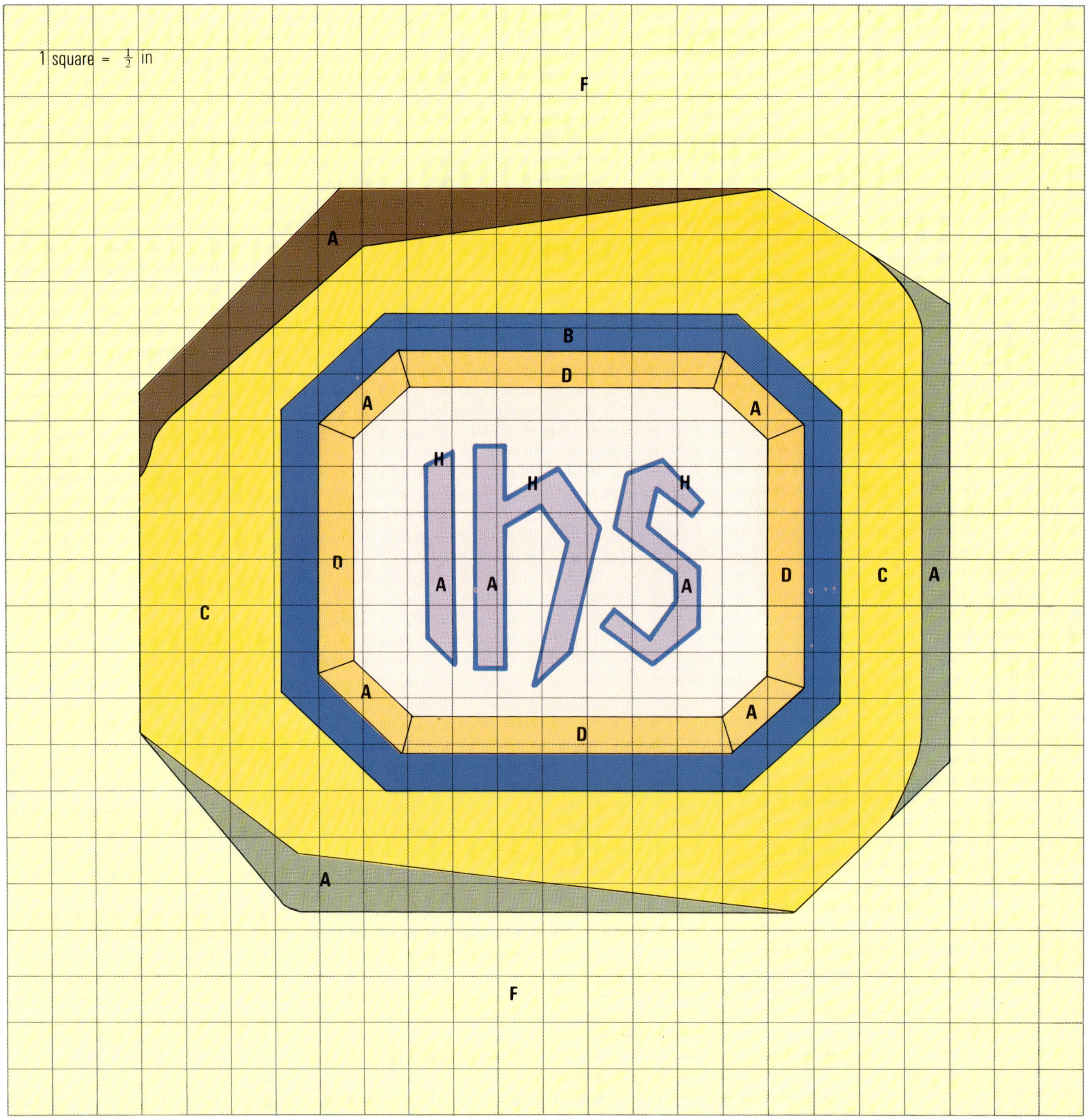

Project three

card for the lining, depending on thickness of total layers of fabrics).

To cover the front and back sections of the burse, first mark the centers both ways on wrong side of embroidery. Lay face down and with centers matching, place card on top. Miter corners and lace across, see page 32.

For the lining, cover two pieces of card with linen, mitering the corners and lacing firmly across, as for fronts.

Spine Fold turnings on spine lining (to make $\frac{3}{4}$ in x width of fronts), and press flat. With wrong sides outside, pin spine over top edges of lining boards, and with matching thread, neatly overcast both sides, see page 32.

Apply adhesive to long piece of card and with canvaswork spine face down, press firmly in place. Fold short ends to wrong side, glue and press. Apply adhesive to long edges of spine and with wrong sides together, place over lining boards pressing firmly in position.

Burse Apply adhesive to wrong side of all four boards, and with corners even, press front and back sections to lining boards. Using matching thread, invisibly slipstitch the top edges to the spine, see page 32. Finally, and also with matching thread, work a buttonhole bar across the center of each side of the burse. This enables it to stand in an upright position, when the embroidery will clearly be seen.

Chalice veil Make a single $\frac{1}{2}$ in turning all round the linen square. Miter corners and press to right side making a sharp fold line on edge. Make $\frac{1}{2}$ in turnings on canvaswork borders and press to wrong side. Make similar turnings on canvaswork corners, mitering each corner and pressing to wrong side. Mark center of veil edges and borders. Open up one side of fold line on border and fold line on veil. With fold lines and centers matching, pin right side of border to wrong side of veil. Machine stitch across and repeat for remaining borders. Similarly, tack the corners in position matching fold lines and corners. Machine stitch around two outer edges of corner. Trim across corners, turn both corners and borders to right side. With matching thread, slipstitch around canvaswork corners and borders. Using matching thread decorate with pearls as shown, slipping needle between canvas and linen.

Burse Back Color Key

Anchor stranded embroidery thread

☐ 0390	☐ 0120	◼ 0143

Crewel yarn

☐ Heraldic gold 1	◼ Brown grounding 4
☐ Heraldic gold 4	☐ Gold cord
☐ Elephant grey 3	

Chalice veil Color Key

Anchor stranded embroidery thread

◼ 0143

Crewel yarn

☐ Heraldic gold 4	☐ Gold cord

Measurement and cutting layout for canvas

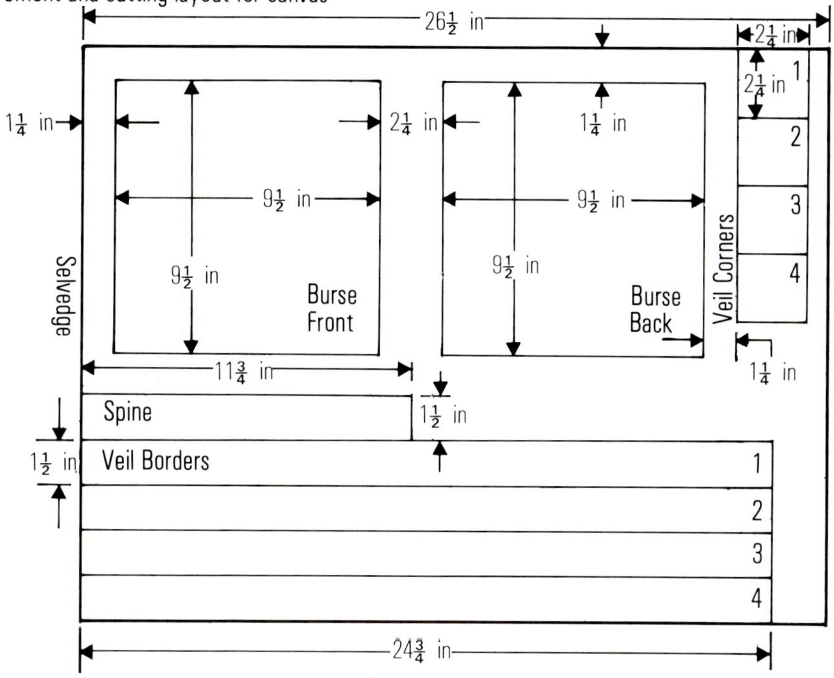

Measurement and cutting layout for linen

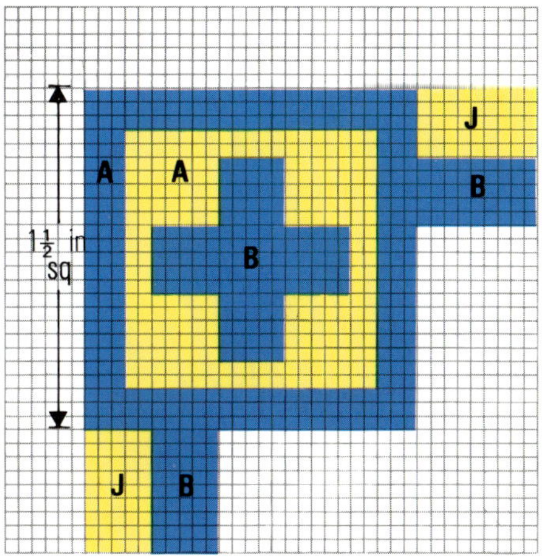

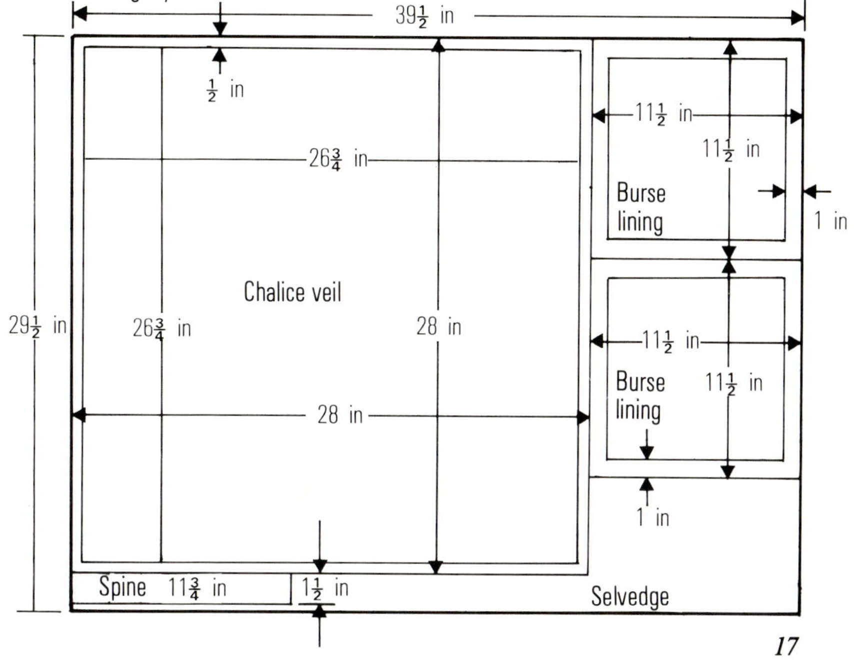

Detail of veil corner
1 square = 1 tent stitch

Chalice veil

Fleur-de-lis Kneeler

Embroider this classically designed kneeler in a range of pinks and blue using a variety of stitches to give an all-over textured effect. The sides of the kneeler are worked in a checker-board pattern of tent and basket stitches, and the edges finished with satin stitch or long armed cross stitch.

Size

10 in x 15 in x 3 in

Materials

$23\frac{1}{2}$ in of $26\frac{3}{4}$ in-wide double canvas with 10 holes to 1 in.
Anchor tapestry yarn in the following amounts and colors: 10 skeins light blue 0508; 3 skeins dull pink 068; 2 skeins pink 067; 1 skein each cream 0386, pale pink 0892, dark pink 0870 and 42 skeins dark blue 0132 for background
10 in x 15 in x 3 in deep of compressed foam
30 in x $32\frac{1}{4}$ in of unbleached calico
17 in x 12 in of suede, leather or imitation leather, for base
Slate frame with $26\frac{3}{4}$ in tapes
Size 20 tapestry needle
Three sided leather needle
Synthetic wadding (optional)
Linen thread

Stitches and techniques

For the following stitches and techniques, see pages 22, 23, 24, 26, 31, and 32.

Diagonal tent stitch
Gobelin stitch
Horizontal mosaic stitch
Long armed cross stitch
Rice stitch
Wheatsheaf stitch
Basket stitch
Blocking the canvas
Covering the kneeler with calico
Lacing the back of the kneeler

Instructions

Using a waterproof marker or colored tacking threads, mark the center of the canvas both ways. Then, following the measurement diagram given opposite mark the outline of the kneeler counting the threads evenly from the center. Stretch the canvas into the frame, see page 30, or if you intend working in the hand, either hem the edges or cover them with masking tape. This prevents the canvas from fraying and the yarn from catching.

Embroidery

Use single tapestry yarn throughout. Following the color and stitch charts given opposite, begin the embroidery with the fleur-de-lis placing them in cross formation as shown. Working outwards from the middle, fill in the background with diagonal tent stitch, leaving the unworked border (two holes wide) around top edge and corner seams. Work the zigzag corner patterns first with wheatsheaf stitch and then fill in with tent stitch to complete the kneeler top. Now, work the side sections in basket stitch and tent stitch blocks,

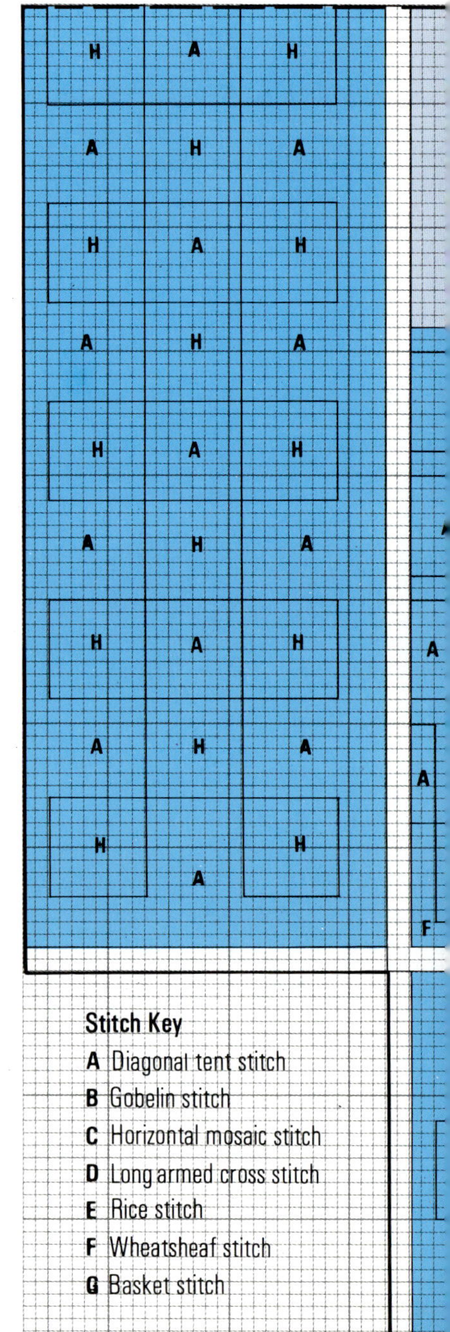

filling in background with tent stitch. Remove completed embroidery from frame and if necessary, block the canvas, see page 31.

Making up

The canvas should be completely dry before cutting out and making up. Cut out the kneeler adding a ¾ in seam allowance all round. With right sides inside, pin and tack together the two side sections at each corner. Using strong thread, stab stitch each seam stitching one hole away from canvaswork. Trim seams, cut across corners and turn through. Press seams open.

Neaten the edges of the kneeler by working long armed cross stitch in dark blue, around the top edge and down each corner seam.

Cover the foam pad with calico, see page 32. Insert pad into kneeler, adding extra wadding to fill out corners if necessary. Fold canvas turnings under base, creasing the edges firmly. Lace edges of canvas across back of kneeler, see page 32. To cover the base with leather or a substitute fabric, first make 1 in turnings all round, mitering corners neatly. Hold in place with a single thread tied through both fabrics in the center of each side of the kneeler. With matching thread in the needle, hem in place. Remove holding threads to finish. A three-sided leather needle is recommended for stitching firm leather since it makes a less obvious hole than ordinary needles. Alternative stitches, such as herringbone stitch and three-sided stitch could also be used, when turning may not be necessary.

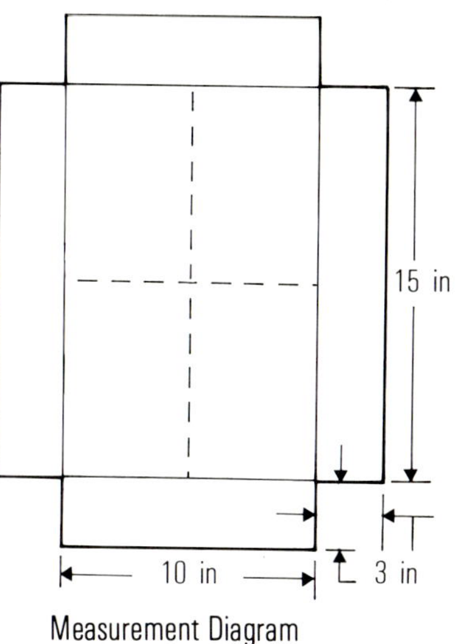

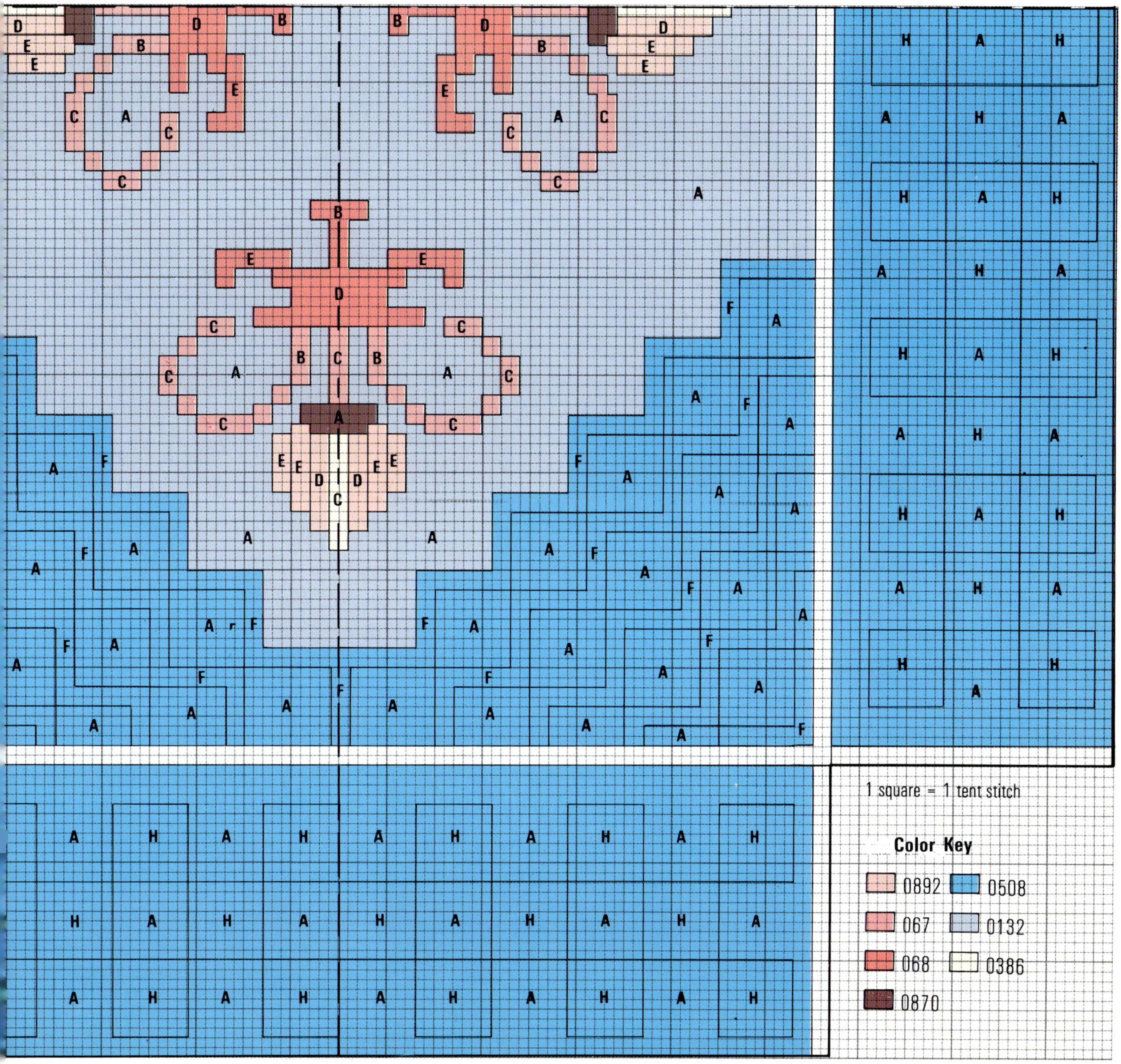

center line

Canvaswork stitches

The great advantage of canvaswork is that it combines making a superb fabric with original design. Designs are worked on to a ready-made canvas and may be embroidered in a variety of colors and stitches with wide textural contrasts.

For successful canvaswork, it is important to match exactly the thickness of yarn to the canvas mesh, with the most suitable stitch. If the canvas mesh is not completely filled, the resulting fabric will look mean and disappointing, and the canvas threads will probably show through the stitching. To correct this, it is usually sufficient to use either a thicker yarn or a smaller canvas mesh, or both.

Good results also involve stitching with an even tension throughout so that the individual stitches show up clearly, giving a solid, firm-textured fabric that will wear well. Before you begin a project, it is always advisable to work a trial sample first, when any adjustments can be made.

Canvas

Embroidery canvases are produced in a variety of widths and in many sizes, in either single (mono) or double thread (Penelope), in a color range of white, cream or brown. The threads of single canvas are counted over a set measurement of 1 in (from 10 to 24 threads) whereas on double canvas, the holes between the pairs of threads are counted over the same measurement (10, 11 and 12 holes). One of the advantages of working on double canvas is that the pairs of threads can be split and worked singly to describe fine detail, thus making 10 double into 20 single canvas, and so on. The threads can be converted to single (simply by pressing them apart with the needle) either all over the design or in specific areas such as very fine lines, or for shading naturalistic foliage, faces and hands. Double canvas is also used extensively for working specific stitches including cross stitch, trammed gros point and Aubusson stitch.

Lockweave canvases are woven with two threads which are twisted or 'locked' together and are worked as single canvases. Lockweave canvases are produced in a restricted variety of widths and sizes, and in white only.

Choose a good quality canvas made from strong linen or polished cotton threads. Better quality canvases are heavier and more firmly woven than cheaper varieties and therefore do not easily allow the stitching to pull the mesh out of shape. However, certain types of diagonal stitches are more prone to distorting the canvas than others. For these stitches, working in a frame is especially recommended.

Evenweave fabrics

Canvaswork stitches can be embroidered equally well on any evenweave fabric, bearing in mind of course, that the more threads there are to 1 in, the finer the stitching will be.

Depending on what the finished article is to be used for, linen ground fabrics worked with either single crewel yarn, soft embroidery, coton à broder, pearl and stranded threads are recommended.

Threads

For kneelers, chair seats and cushions that are expected to receive a great deal of hard wear, a strong pure wool is recommended for the embroidery. Wool is not only a strong and hardwearing fiber, it has an unusual facility for 'wearing clean'. For working your own designs, choose either carpet weaving wool, tapestry yarn, crewel or stranded Persian yarn. All these yarns may be doubled in the needle, or the number of strands increased, to give a denser coverage. Choose pearl, stranded and soft embroidery thread for matt effects, and silk, rayon and metallic thread for highlights.

Crewel wool

This is a fine, firmly twisted 2-ply yarn which can be used singly on the finest canvas, or in multiple strands on coarser canvases. It is available in a wide range of colors.

Tapestry wool

This is a softly-twisted, single yarn equivalent in thickness to a fingering knitting weight. It is made in a comprehensive range of designer's colors.

Persian yarn

This is a 3-stranded yarn, made up of 2-ply strands loosely twisted together. The strands can be worked singly or in multiple strands as required, with plain or mixed colors in the needle. There is a good selection of colors.

Carpet wool or thrums

This is carpet weaving/knotting wool which is a thick 2-ply yarn equivalent to a coarse sportweight. These yarns are particularly hardwearing. They are mothproof and can be bought by the hank or, as thrums, which are mixed offcuts from carpet looms. The color range is limited.

Needles

Round-pointed tapestry needles are especially made for embroidering on canvas. They have a long eye for carrying thick yarns, and can be bought in sizes ranging from 13 to 24. There are no set rules governing which needle to use with which canvas, but generally speaking, the needle should be slightly thicker than the working thread. It should be small enough to pass easily through the canvas without forcing the threads apart and have a sufficiently large eye to take the yarn.

Beginning to stitch and fastening off

Make a knot at the end of the yarn and insert the needle several threads away from the starting point. Continue to work in pattern over the yarn. Leave the knot on the surface until the work is finished and then trim the knot away. Subsequent new yarn can be started by running it through the back of the completed stitches.

Fasten off by running the needle under the last three or four stitches on the wrong side, before cutting the yarn.

Diagonal stitches

Diagonal stitches in general cover the canvas mesh well, and are very hardwearing. Small stitches, such as tent and Gobelin stitch, are ideal for describing the fine details of a design, especially in realistic coloring, and as flat backgrounds on which to show chunkier stitches in high relief. Choose longer diagonal stitches to express changes of movement, and shading.

Horizontal tent stitch

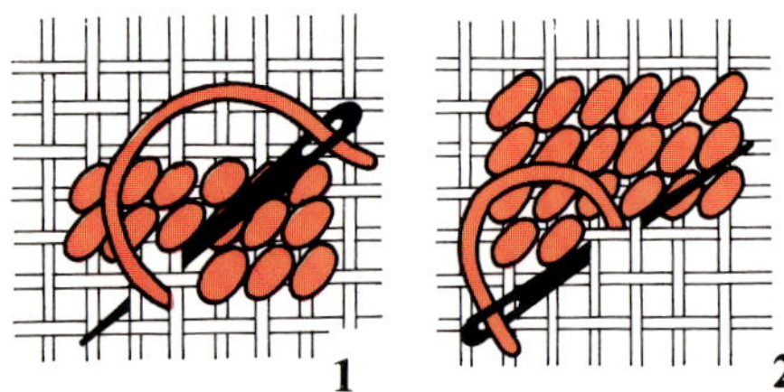

1 Bring out the yarn at top right, insert the needle diagonally upwards over one intersection and bring it out one thread down and two threads to left. Continue to end of row.
2 Work the second row from left to right passing the needle diagonally upwards. All stitches should slope in the same direction.

Diagonal tent stitch

This method of working tent stitch is recommended for all large areas, since it does reduce the risk of the finished canvas being pulled out of shape.

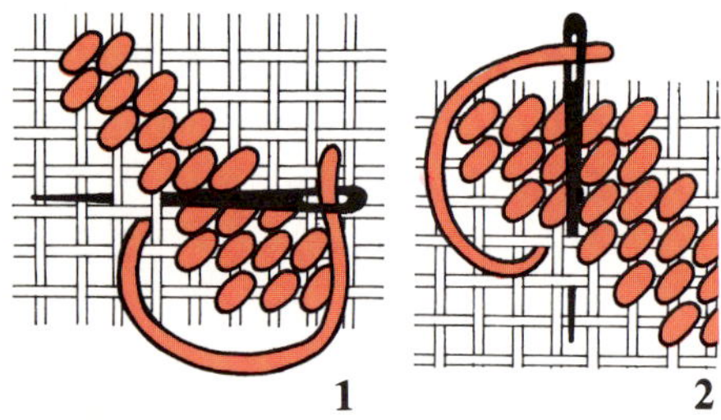

1 Bring yarn out to left and insert the needle upwards over one intersection, pass needle behind two vertical threads and bring out ready to make the next stitch. Continue to end of row.
2 Work the next row downwards. First insert the needle upwards over one intersection, pass it downwards behind two horizontal threads and bring out. Continue to end of row. Notice how the stitches fit neatly into the spaces of the previous row.

Gros point

This stitch is best worked on double canvas and when trammed with an underpadding, is an excellent stitch for kneelers and chair seats.

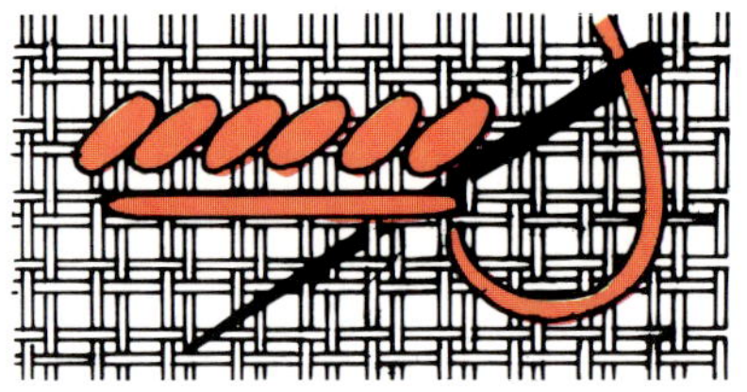

Bring out the yarn in between the double threads. Make a long stitch to the right (not more than $1\frac{1}{4}$ in — $1\frac{1}{2}$ in) and bring the needle out just below, one double thread to left. Insert needle diagonally upwards over the double intersection, pass needle behind and bring out one double thread down and two to left.

Gobelin stitch

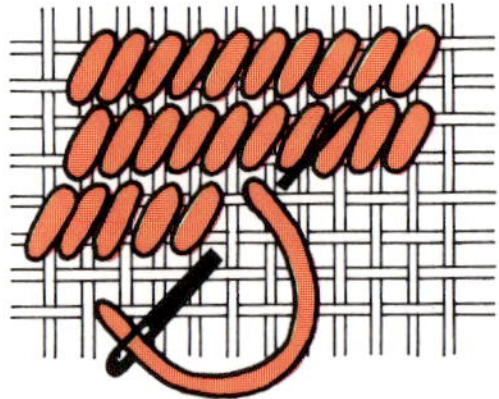

Working in horizontal rows, bring the yarn out to left. Make a diagonal stitch downwards over two threads and one thread to left. Pass needle behind and bring out two threads up and one to right. Repeat to end of row and work the next and subsequent rows below alternating from right to left and vice versa.

Diagonal Stitch

Encroaching Gobelin stitch

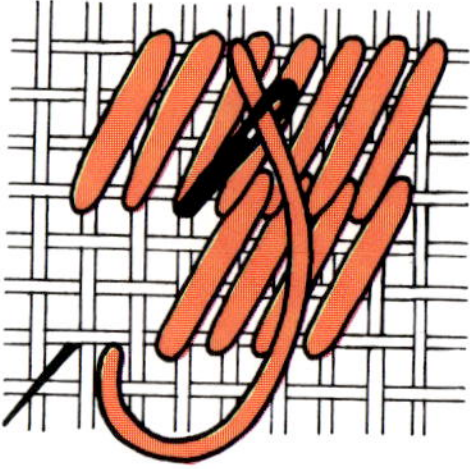

Bring needle out, make a row of diagonal stitches upwards over four threads and two threads to right. Work the second row in the same way overlapping the previous row by one horizontal thread.

Diagonal stitch

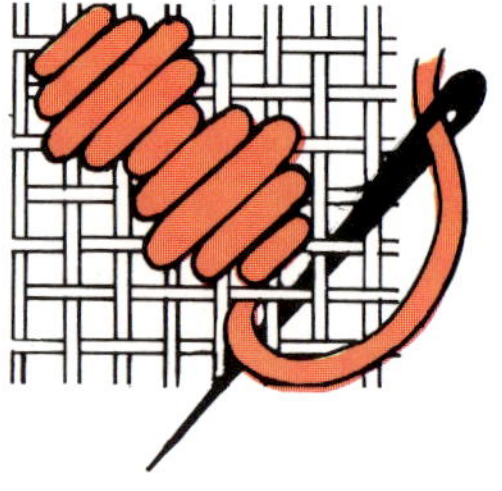

Working from top left to bottom right, make a series of diagonal stitches in sequence over two, three, four and three intersections of thread. Work the following rows below, placing the longest stitches diagonally in line with the shortest stitches of the previous row.

Aubusson stitch

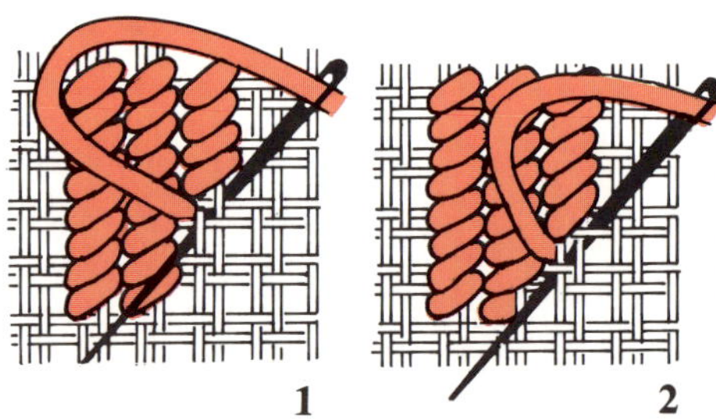

1 Bring yarn through at top left in between a horizontal double thread. Insert needle diagonally to right over one vertical double thread and bring out in the space below the starting point.
2 Make a second diagonal stitch, inserting the needle in between the horizontal double thread to right and bringing it through in between the horizontal double thread down to left.

Cashmere stitch

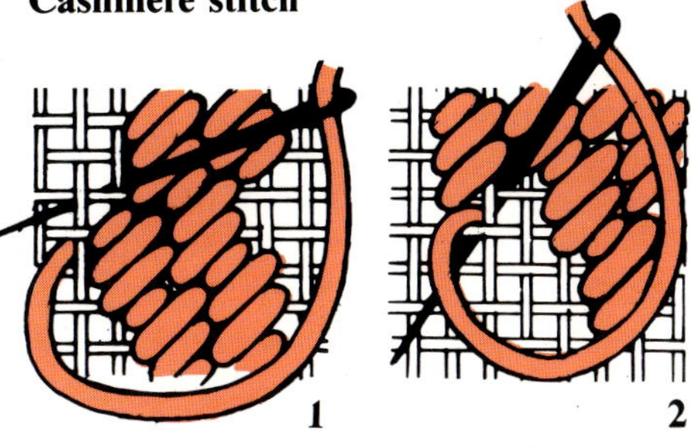

1 Working from bottom right to top left, make a series of diagonal stitches in sequence over one, two, and two intersections of thread, placing each group of stitches one thread to left as shown.
2 Work the next row in the oppposite direction following the same sequence, moving each group of stitches one thread to the left.

Horizontal mosaic stitch

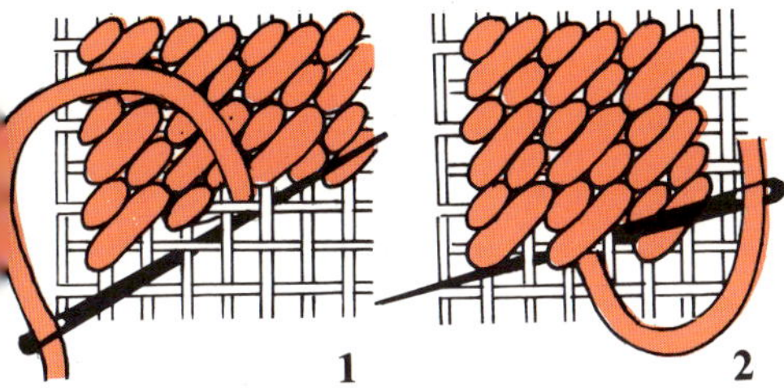

1 Working from left to right, bring needle out at top left and make a series of diagonal stitches over one, and two intersections of thread. Continue to end of row.
2 Work the next row from right to left, working small diagonal stitches into the spaces left on the previous row. Repeat steps 1 and 2.

Diagonal mosaic stitch

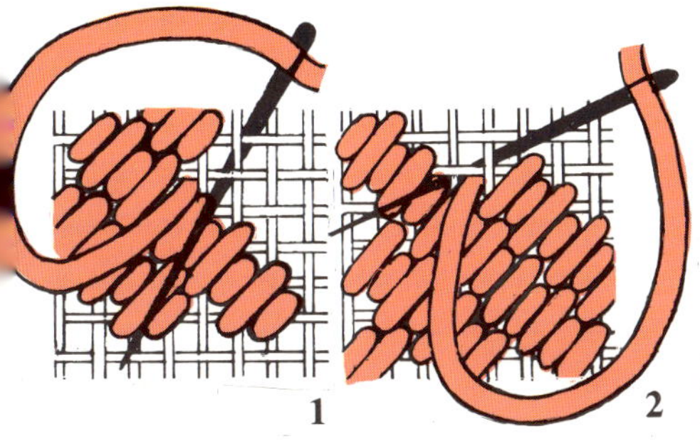

1 Working from top left to bottom right, bring yarn out to left and make a series of diagonal stitches to right, alternately over one and two intersections of thread. Complete the first row.
2 Work the second row in the opposite direction, neatly placing the longest stitch in line with the shortest stitch of the previous row.

Chequer stitch

This stitch consists of a series of alternating squares of diagonal stitch and tent stitch worked over four intersections of thread.

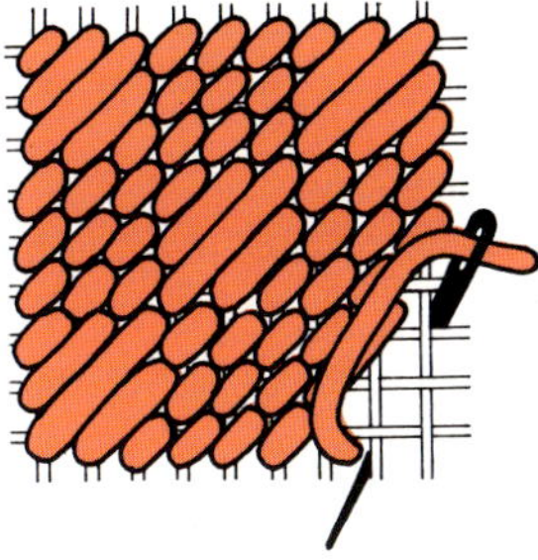

Begin at the top left, and working diagonally downwards, complete the squares of tent stitch first. Then, fill in the remaining squares with diagonal stitches in sequence over one, two, three, two and one intersections of thread.

Scottish Stitch

Byzantine stitch

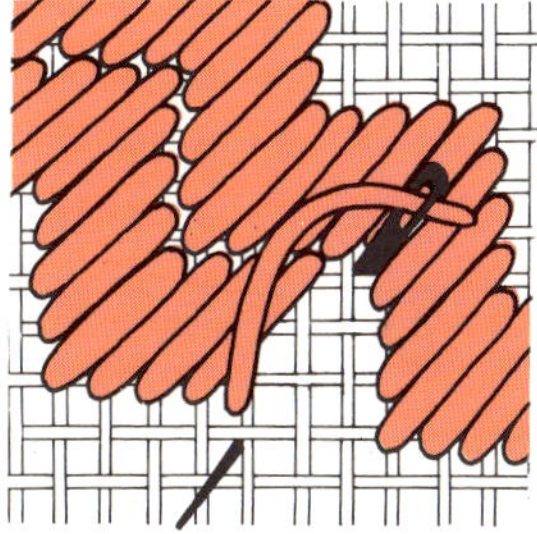

Begin at the bottom right and work four diagonal stitches to the left over three intersections of thread, followed by four diagonal stitches worked vertically over three intersections of thread. Continue in this way, repeating the step pattern.

Scottish stitch

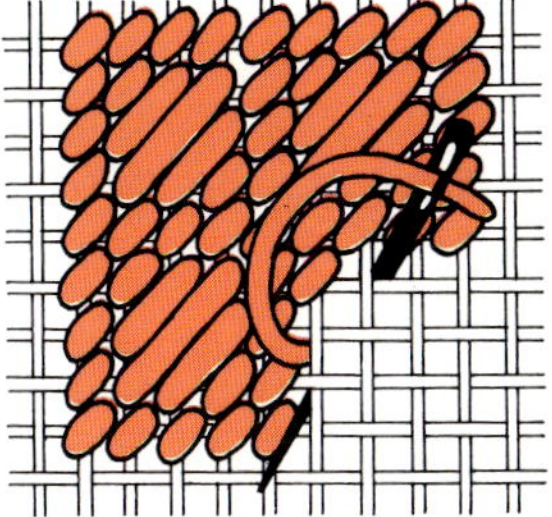

Working horizontally from left to right, begin by outlining the squares with tent stitch. Embroider the horizontal rows first, stitching every fifth row, then work the vertical rows to complete the outlining. Fill in the squares with diagonal stitches working in sequence over one, two, three, two and one intersections of thread.

Cushion stitch

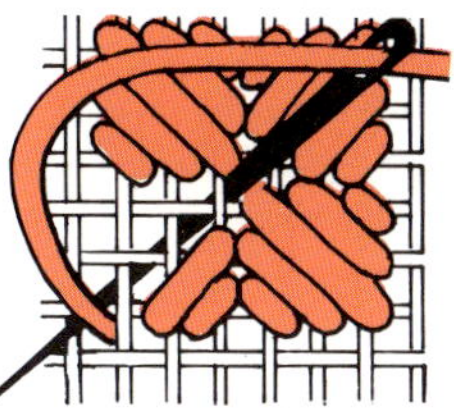

Working horizontally from right to left, make a square of diagonal stitches worked in sequence over one, two, three, two and one intersections of thread. For the following squares, either repeat the same square throughout or work the next and every alternate square with the stitches slanting in the opposite direction, as shown in the diagram.

Knitting stitch

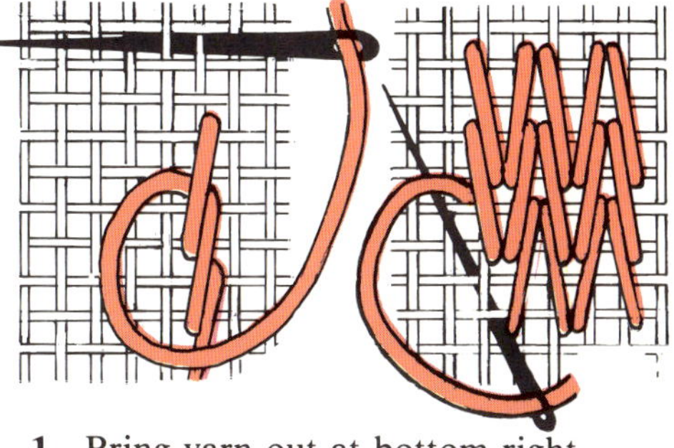

1 Bring yarn out at bottom right, insert needle four threads up and one to right, and bring out two threads down and one to left. Continue to end of row bringing needle out two threads to left ready to work the next row downwards in reverse.
2 Insert needle four threads down and one to right. Bring out two threads up and one to left. Repeat as before.

Crossed stitches

Crossed stitches are by their nature well padded and are therefore by far the most hardwearing group of stitches. Worked on canvas, they are particularly useful for upholstered items such as chair seats, kneelers and stool covers. In addition to the standard cross stitch, there are many other attractively textured and distinctive variations. For a neat and regular appearance, make sure that all the stitches cross in the same direction.

Cross stitch

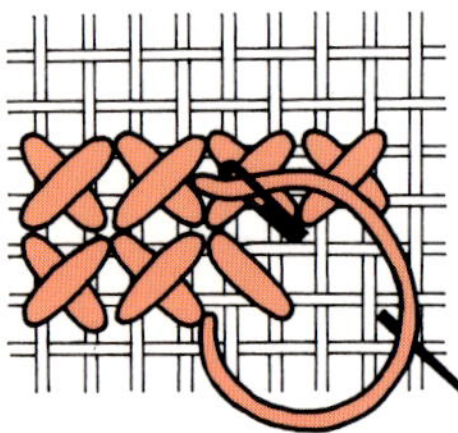

Working horizontally from right to left, bring the needle out, insert it upwards over two intersections of thread to the left and bring out two horizontal threads below. Re-insert it diagonally upwards over two intersections to right and bring out at the starting point. Repeat to end of row. Work the return row in reverse, as shown in the diagram.

Long armed cross stitch

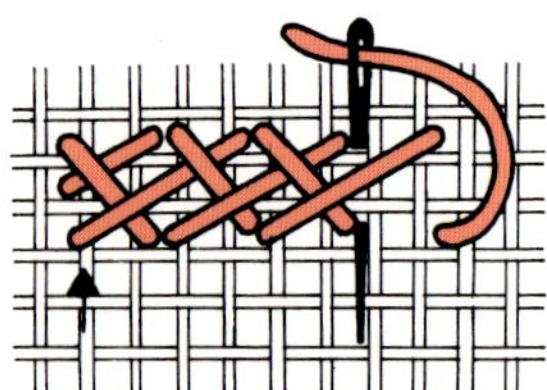

Work in horizontal rows from left to right. Bring yarn out, make a diagonal stitch over four intersections of thread to right and bring needle out two threads down. Make a second diagonal stitch over two intersections to left and bring needle out two threads below. Repeat to end of row.

Double cross stitch

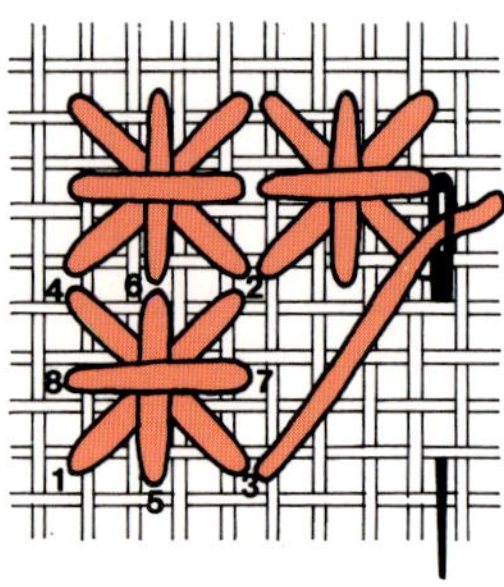

Working from left to right, first make a cross stitch over four intersections of thread bringing the needle out at 5, as in diagram. Then work an upright cross on top following the numbers given, bringing the needle out at 3 ready to work the next stitch.

Rice stitch

This stitch is often worked both in two thicknesses of yarn and in two colours.

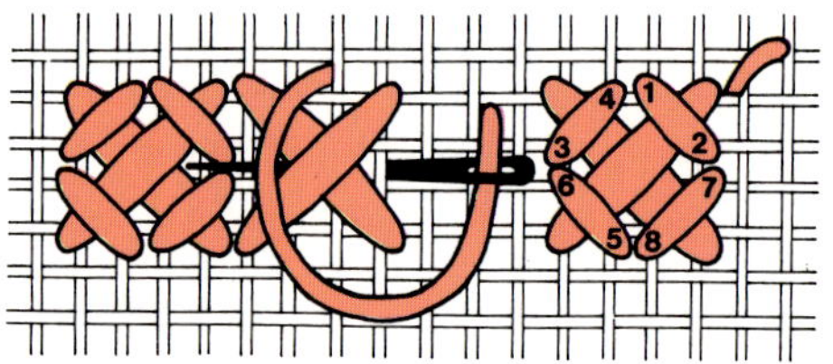

With thicker yarn in needle, begin at top left, and working to the right, work a row of cross stitches over four intersections of thread. With a thinner contrasting thread in the needle (optional) and making diagonal stitches over two intersections, tie down the corners of each cross following the number sequence as shown in the diagram.

Wheatsheaf stitch

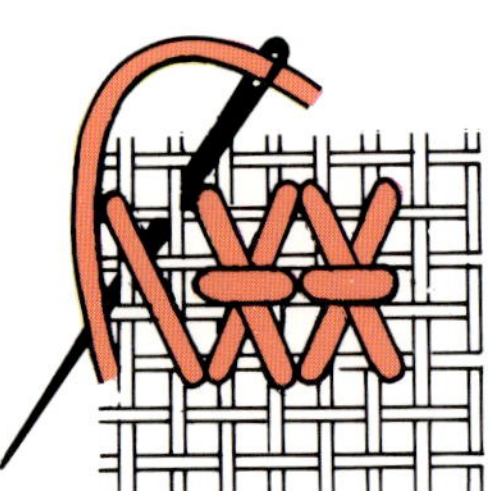

Bring yarn out at top left, and working to right, make a cross stitch over four horizontal and two vertical threads, bringing needle out two threads below starting point. Re-insert needle two threads to right and bring out two threads up, ready to make the next stitch.

Knotted stitch

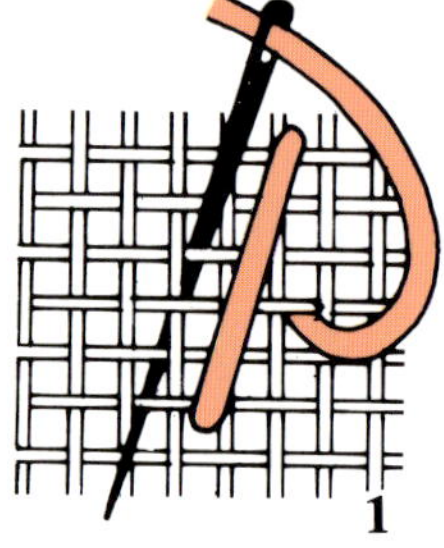
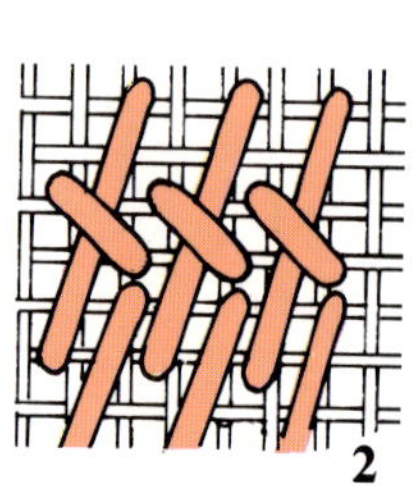

1 Working horizontal rows from right to left, bring yarn out and insert needle six threads up and two to right, bringing needle out four threads down. Make a diagonal stitch upwards over two intersections and bring needle out four threads down and one to left of starting point. Continue to end of row.
2 Work next and subsequent rows below bringing needle out four threads down and overlapping the previous row by two horizontal threads.

Dutch cross stitch

Embroider the wide cross stitches first, working over four vertical and two horizontal threads. Fit the second row into the first as shown, in diamond formation. To complete the cross, bring the needle out in the middle one thread above the cross, and take it down over four threads. Bring needle out as shown ready to complete the next cross.

Norwich Stitch

Velvet Stitch (trimmed)

Rhodes stitch

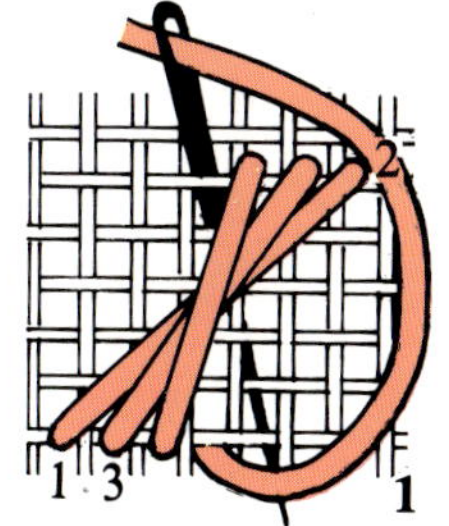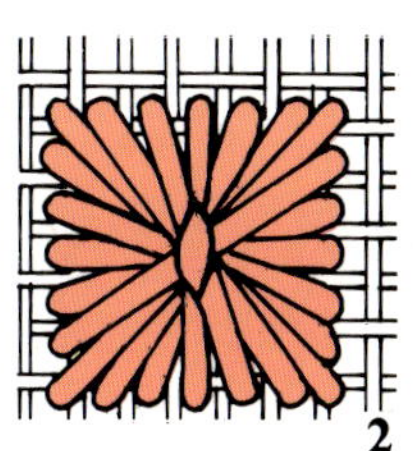

1 Begin at bottom left and make a series of diagonal stitches to cover a square of six vertical and six horizontal threads. With yarn at bottom left 1, insert needle at 2 and bring out at 3. Continue in this way to fill the square.

2 Finish by tying the crossed threads with an upright stitch worked in the middle over two horizontal threads.

Star stitch

This stitch forms a square over four vertical and four horizontal threads.

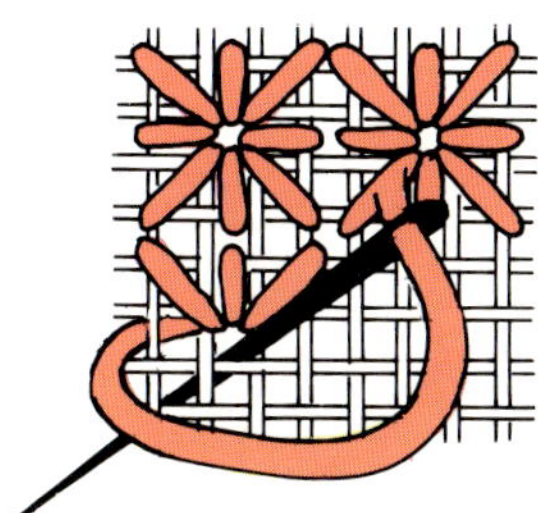

Begin at top right and working inwards from the outer edge, work straight stitches so as to form an eight-pointed star. Work each stitch over two thread intersections, each radiating from the same central point as shown. Continue to end of row and repeat as required.

Velvet stitch

This stitch imitates the pile of oriental carpets and may be left either as loops or trimmed to form a close-cut pile.

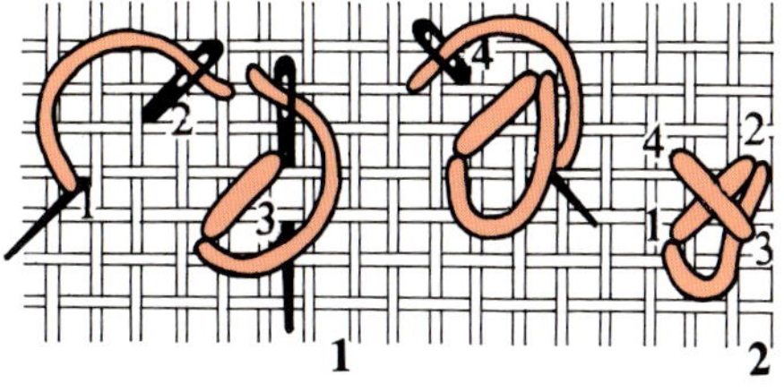

1 With a reasonably thick yarn in the needle, and working from left to right, bring needle out at bottom left. Make a diagonal stitch over two intersections of thread. Bring needle out at starting point and repeat leaving a loop of yarn as shown. Bring needle out two threads below at 3.

2 Insert needle diagonally to 4 and bring out at 3 to begin the next stitch.

Star stitches

Radiating star stitches are relatively easy to work. They cover the ground quickly, giving rich decorative textures. Eyelets also combine very well with other square stitches to give interesting all-over patterns. While both leaf and Rhodes stitch cover the canvas mesh well, it is often necessary to work back stitches between other star stitches to completely cover the mesh.

Eye stitch

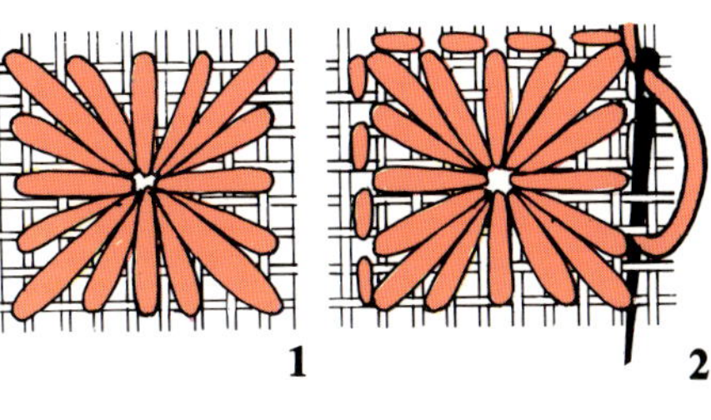

1 Begin at top right corner of star and work a series of 16 straight stitches, all radiating from the same central point, and covering eight vertical and eight horizontal threads. Leave two threads between each stitch.

2 Complete required number of eyelets, and with the same or contrast yarn, outline them with back stitches worked over two threads.

Norwich stitch

These large decorative squares are worked over an uneven number of threads.

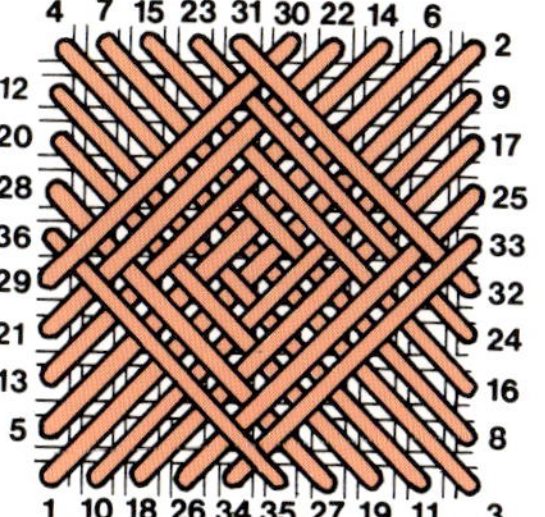

Begin with a long length of yarn in the needle, about 32 in — 40 in, and work diagonal stitches following the number sequence given in the diagram until the last round of stitches. Slip the needle under stitches 30, 32, 34 and 36, and then take it through to the back to finish.

Fan stitch

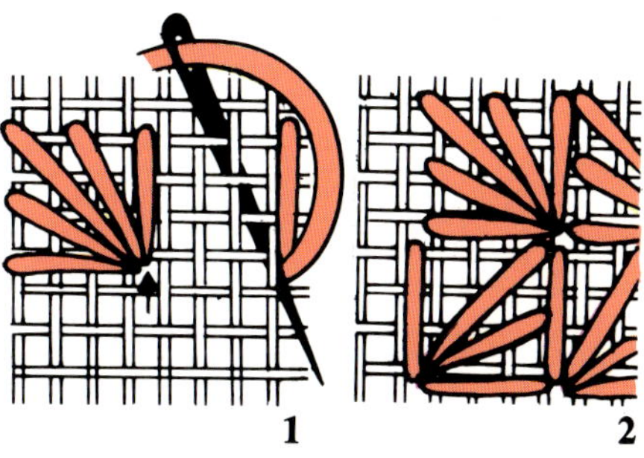

1 Beginning at the arrow, insert the needle four threads up and bring out at starting point. Continue in this way to make a series of five straight stitches radiating from the same point and with two threads between each stitch.

2 Work the next and every other row in the opposite direction starting with the upright thread of the fan.

Straight stitches

Of all the canvaswork stitches, these are the simplest to work adding subtle changes of texture to the embroidery. You will see how quickly straight stitch patterns can be made and how fast they cover the canvas without distorting it. Remember that very long stitches will snag and are less hardwearing than shorter stitches. Under padding with a laid thread (tramming) is recommended for some stitches such as upright Gobelin stitch.

Counted satin stitch

This stitch may be worked vertically or horizontally in bands or blocks, or a mixture of both.

For horizontal bands, bring yarn out, insert needle upwards over four threads and bring out one thread to right ready to work the next stitch. Continue to end of row and repeat as shown.

Basket stitch

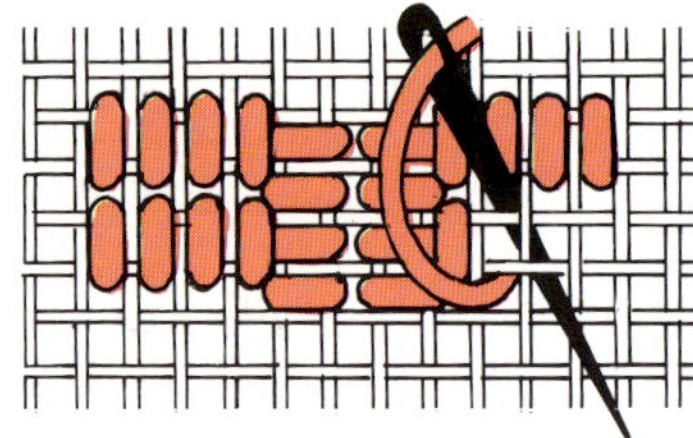

Working horizontally from left to right, embroider pairs of blocks of counted satin stitch alternately over two horizontal and two vertical threads. For a closely woven finish, place the first and fourth stitches of each block neatly into the same holes as the previous blocks.

Twill filling stitch

This stitch is particularly suitable for large single canvas and thick yarn.

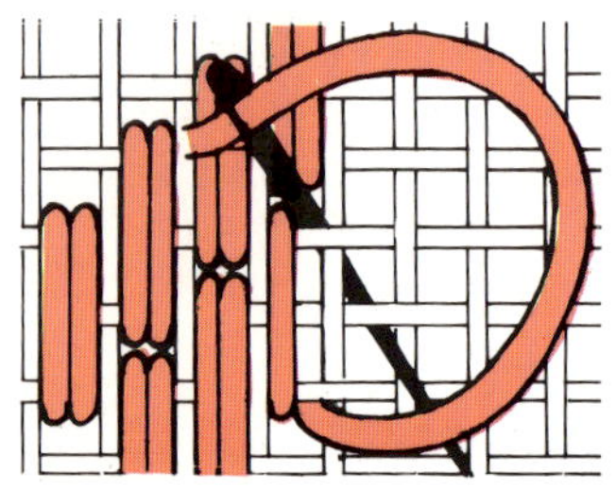

Begin at bottom left and working diagonally upwards, make pairs of stepped straight stitches three threads up and back two, working the two stitches into the same hole as shown. Continue to end of row and repeat following rows below.

Hungarian stitch

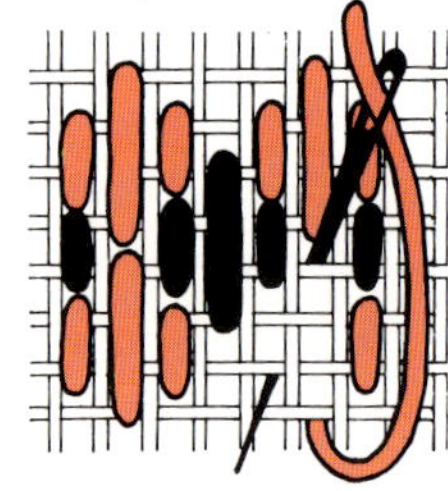

Working in horizontal rows, make groups of three vertical stitches over two, four and two horizontal threads of canvas. Leave two vertical threads between each group. Work the return journey in the same way fitting the stitches neatly into the spaces made by previous row.

Hungarian stitch

Upright Gobelin stitch

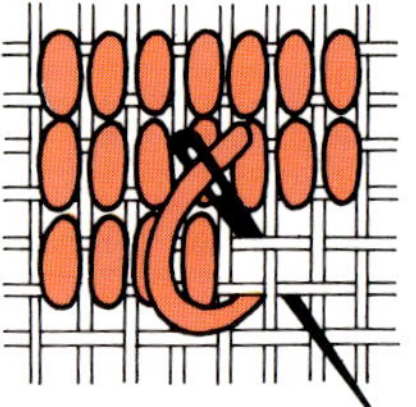

Working in horizontal rows from left to right and vice versa, bring needle out, insert it two threads above and bring out one thread along. Repeat to end of row. To prevent the canvas mesh from showing between the rows, this stitch should be worked over a laid thread, (see Gros point on page 22).

Parisian stitch

Begin at top left and work straight stitches alternately upwards over six and two threads to end of row. Work the return journey in the same way alternating the length of the stitches to fit evenly into the previous row.

Algerian filling stitch

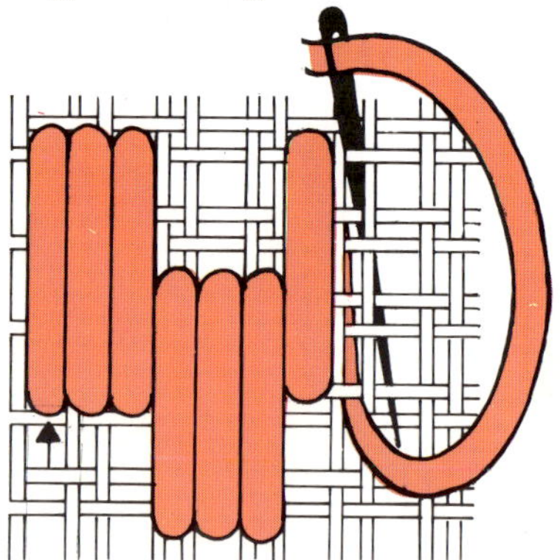

Working on double canvas, begin at the left in between a double thread, and make three upright stitches over six threads. Bring needle out three threads below and one to right. Work a similar block of stitches bringing the needle out three threads above and one to right, and repeat. Continue in this way, working following rows in an opposite direction and fitting the stitches evenly into the previous row.

Gobelin filling stitch

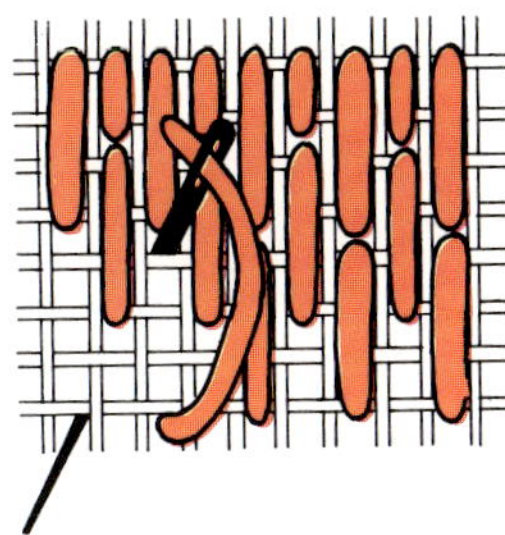

Begin at top left and work a row of straight stitches upwards over four threads leaving two threads between each one. Work the second row in the opposite direction fitting in the stitches evenly into the previous row. Repeat rows one and two.

Back stitch on canvas

This is an extremely useful stitch for outlining — for defining both color and stitch — and also for covering the canvas mesh between rows, especially where horizontal rows of upright stitches meet. Use either a matching or contrast colored yarn.

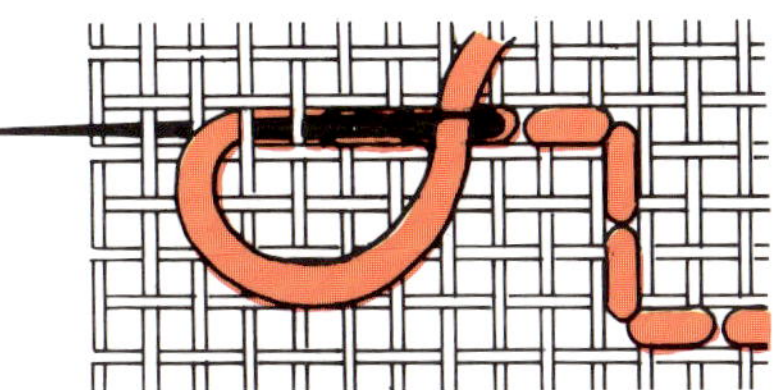

Working from right to left, make a stitch over two threads to right bringing needle out two threads to left. Repeat to end of row.

Florentine stitch

This stitch is traditionally used to show subtle gradations of color, often in every row.

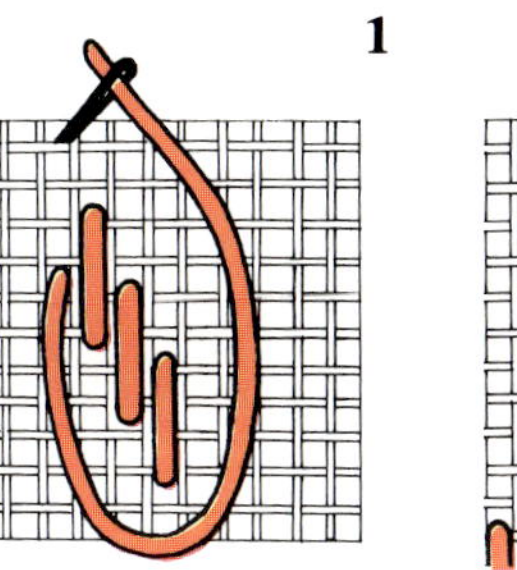 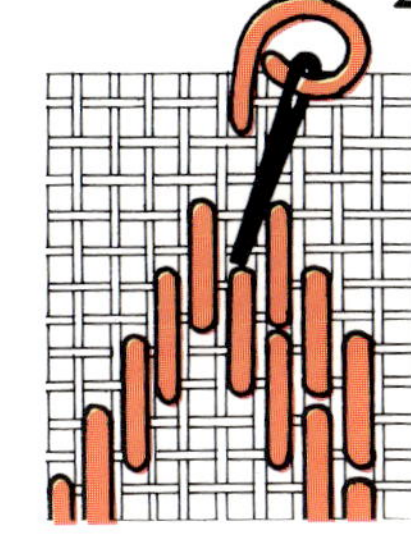

1 Working from bottom right to top left, bring needle out and make five vertical stitches up over four threads and back two. Work four stitches down in reverse and repeat to end of row.
2 Work subsequent rows above, fitting the stitches neatly into the previous row.

Renaissance stitch

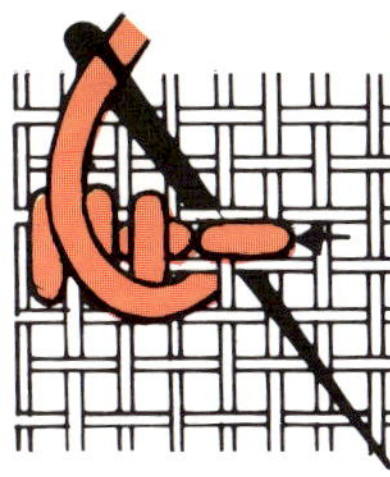 

1 With yarn at arrow, insert needle two threads to left and bring out one thread below. Insert needle two threads up and bring out one thread along.
2 Repeat last stage; bringing needle out below ready to work next stitch.

Long stitch

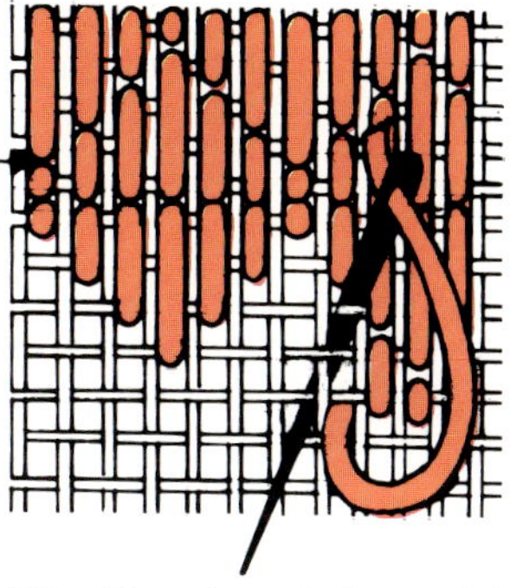

Working from left to right and vice versa, make a series of vertical stitches in sequence over four, three, two, one, two and three threads to form a triangular pattern. Work the second row below in reverse sequence over one, two, three, four, three and two threads to form a band. Repeat the two rows throughout.

Long stitch variation

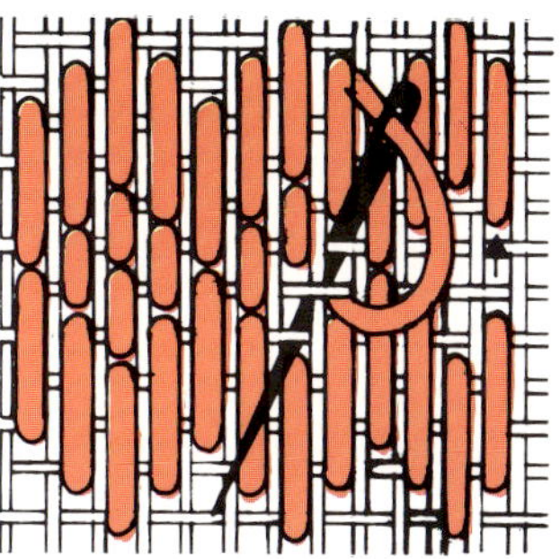

Begin at arrow and work a foundation row in wave pattern repeating three stitches upwards over four threads and two stitches downwards over four. Work a second row in reverse sequence. Fill spaces left with four stitches as shown.

Florentine stitch design worked in reversed pinnacles

Four-way Florentine repeated diagonally in reverse

Techniques

The planning and preparation of any piece of embroidery involves several different elements and skills, from calculating costs to basic design. For successful results, it is best to know something about the basic techniques available.

Working with an embroidery frame

Choose a chair which properly supports your back and always work where there is a good source of light. A standard lamp or angled desk lamp placed close to the frame is most useful in artificial light.

Do not mix odd yarns and threads together; keep in a container only those materials necessary for the work in progress.

Protect the embroidery with a cover when it is not being worked.

Calculating yarn

All the yarns and threads required for the projects are individually specified, but should you wish to design your own piece of canvaswork, the following guide will be useful.

The exact amount of yarn required to cover a given area of canvas varies with the coarseness of the canvas, and with the stitch you plan to use. It is best to work a 1 in square on your chosen canvas, estimate the total area to be stitched and then calculate how much you will need. It is advisable to buy all the yarn at the same time, especially large amounts which should come from the same dye lot.

Calculating canvas

Choose the most appropriate size of mesh and width of canvas best suited to the article you wish to make. After calculating the total amount, add an extra 2 in to 3 in all round for mounting in the frame and for blocking.

Stitching

One of the advantages of working in a frame is that the stitches can correctly be made in two movements, with one hand on top inserting the needle downwards while the other hand returns it from underneath.

For best results, work evenly throughout, keeping the yarn relaxed and correctly twisted, and allowing it to fill the canvas threads completely.

Length of thread

Do not use too long a thread in the needle or it will become worn and thin and will probably break. Even the best wools have flaws and it is false economy to go on using a thread simply because it has just been started. A length of about 15 in to 18 in is generally recommended.

Correcting tightly twisted yarn

As the stitching progresses, the yarn may twist in the needle and become too thin to cover the canvas threads.

Avoid this happening by passing the needle under the yarn with the point downwards, and giving it a half turn to the left, before making the next stitch. Alternatively, lift the canvas and let the needle hang loose, when it will quickly unwind.

Planning the order of stitching

Whenever possible, try to plan the order in which the rows are stitched so that the needle comes up through an empty hole and returns through a filled one.

This gives a smoother finish and sharper definition to the stitch and prevents the needle from splitting the yarn.

Hand-held canvas

If you plan to embroider your canvas in the hand, then working will be made easier if it is rolled. Start from the bottom and roll it to a point close to the central working area and fasten the sides, knotting a length of thread through the mesh. On very long canvases, roll the opposite end as well.

Marking the fabric

Since blocking canvaswork and damp-pressing fabric requires that they are dampened with water, it is most important to use only waterproof markers, or a light pencil or tacking threads. Avoid using felt-tipped pens and biros. These pens are not waterproof and would leave permanent stains on the embroidery if they became wet.

Detail from illustration of Madonna sewing with spring scissors in work basket; School of Bruges c. 1520

Rectangular or slate frame

Although a frame is not an essential piece of equipment, there are many advantages in using one, especially for **canvas** work. A frame keeps the fabric stretched evenly leaving both hands free to work more speedily, and to make stitches with the correct up and down movements.

Slate frames consist of four lengths of wood: two rollers which form the top and bottom and have a length of strong webbing attached, and two stretchers which form the sides of the frame and have a series of holes at each end so that the frame can be adjusted in size. These frames are available in different sizes, from 10 in upwards. The size is measured across the roller tape, which also determines the width of fabric which may be used.

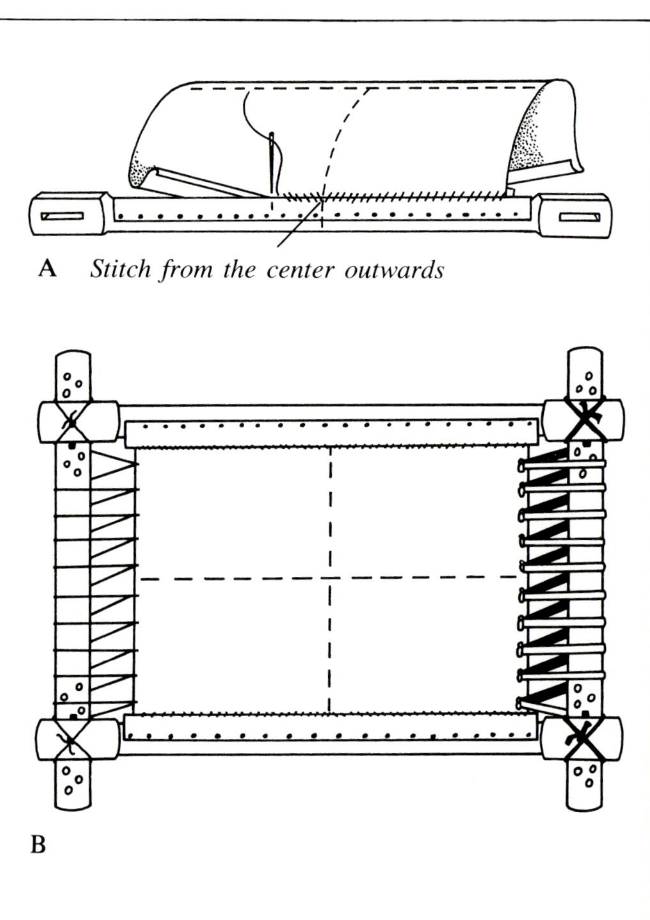

A   *Stitch from the center outwards*

B

Dressing a slate frame

Having marked the center of the canvas both ways, lightly mark the center of both rollers with pencil. Fold $\frac{1}{2}$ in turnings on cut edges of canvas, and with centers matching, pin to webbing. Using a strong thread in the needle, oversew canvas to roller working outwards from the center, as shown in diagram A.

Repeat on the second roller. If required, turn in the selvedges to fit the tapes.

Wind any surplus canvas round one of the rollers adjusting the canvas so that the design to be embroidered is in the middle of the frame. Insert the stretchers and fit the pegs so that the canvas is stretched firmly and evenly. Lace the side edges of canvas with fine string attaching it firmly to the corners of the frame where the rollers and stretchers cross.

For lacing finer fabrics into a slate frame, lengths of flat tape **pinned as on right in diagram B** are recommended.

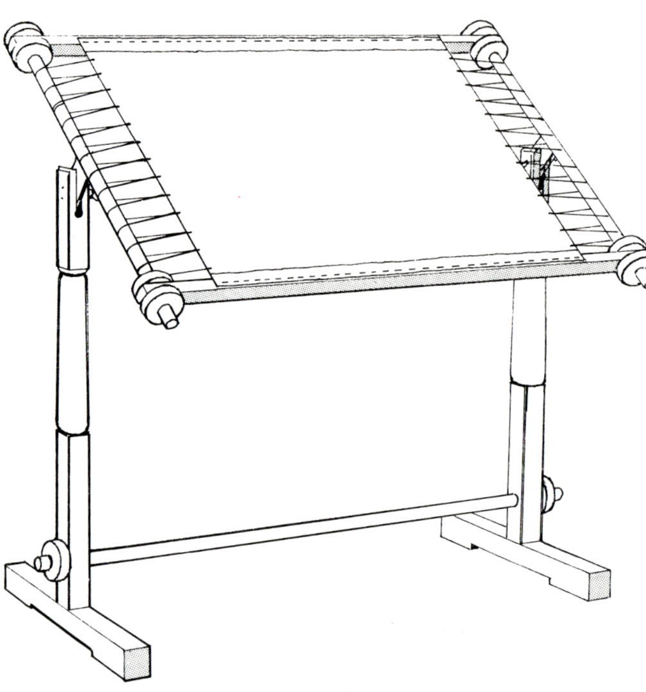

Straight-sided frame with floor stand

This type of frame is lighter in weight than the slate frame previously described. It has two rollers with webbing attached and two threaded stretchers which are adjusted with large circular screw attachments. The cross member on the stand is tightened securely to keep it firm and rigid.

The advantages of working with one of these frames is that no other work table is required and that it can easily be moved to a convenient light source.

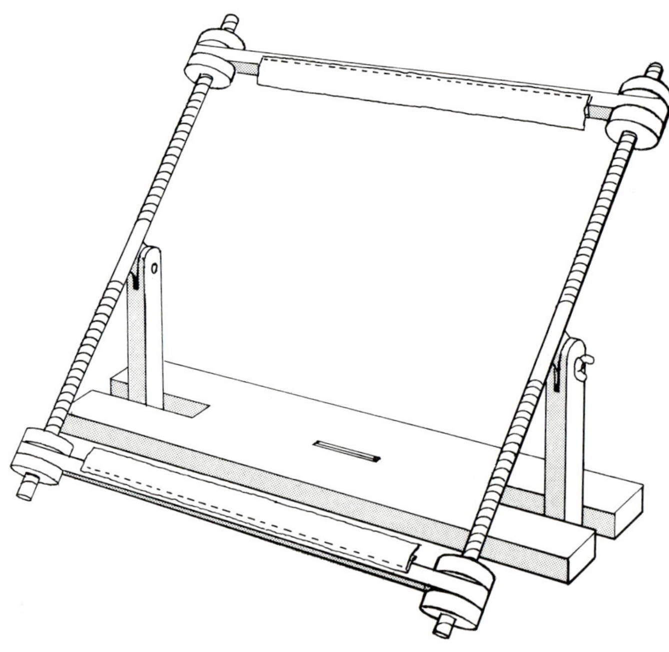

Straight-sided frame with table top stand

This is a smaller frame than the one described above, and is available with 18 in and 24 in tapes. The frame with a table top stand is designed as a compact unit for the convenience of working, particularly in a small work room where it will take up less space than either the floor stand or other necessary side supports for medium to large hand-held frames.

Making your own frame

A home-made frame can be assembled quickly and need not be expensive. It can be made to any size by fastening together four straight pieces of wood in one of the following ways. It is essential that all four corners are right angles.

Mitered joint This is a simple picture frame construction where the ends of the four pieces of wood are cut at 45° angles and secured first with wood glue then pinned through (A).

Butt joint Four straight pieces of wood are butted together at each corner and held in place with an angle iron secured with small screws (B).

Overlapped joint On four pieces of wood, the opposite half section of each corner is measured and cut away. The corners are overlapped and fastened with a counter-sunk screw (C).

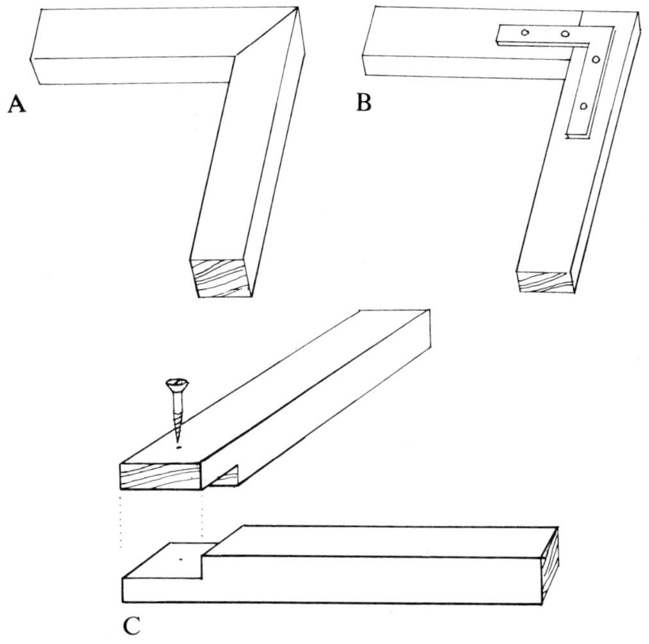

Stretching fabric on a frame

Cut the fabric to size and mark the center of each edge. Mark the wrong side of the frame in the same way. Place frame on wrong side of fabric and with marks matching, staple the center of each side to hold. Pull fabric evenly, and working outwards from the middle, staple to frame leaving corners until last. Fold corners as shown in diagram, and staple to finish.

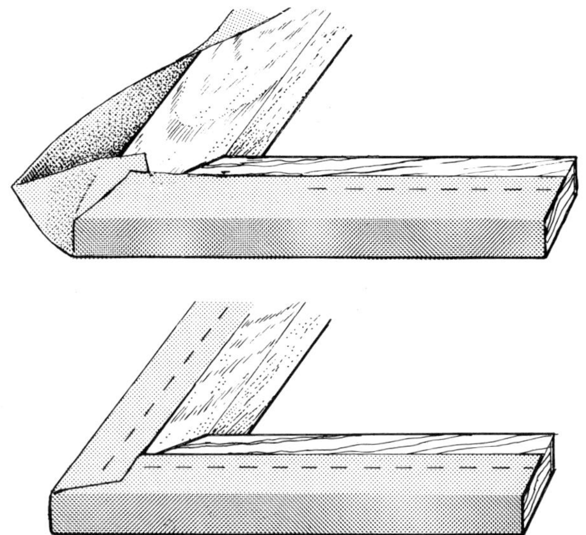

Blocking the canvas

Before making up an article, it is sometimes necessary to stretch the embroidery, either to remove puckers or more usually, to restore canvaswork to its original shape.

Blocking will not alter the size of an embroidery but it will correct any distortion and give it that smooth, even look of new fabric. Should a piece of canvaswork be badly out of shape, then it may require blocking a second time.

It is important not to trim away the margins around the embroidery until the blocking has been completed.

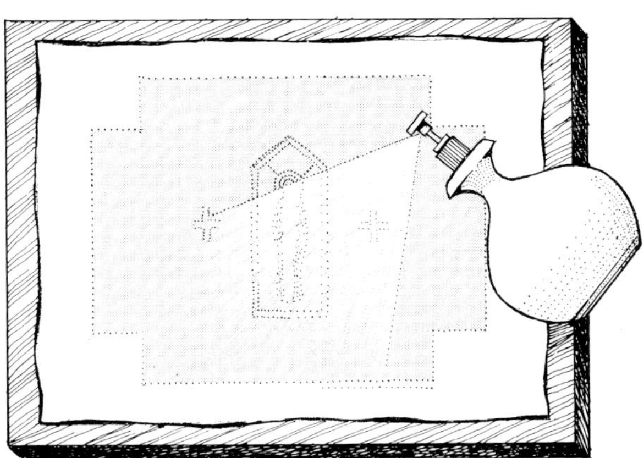

Working on a wooden board, dampen the back of the embroidery with a sponge or spray to soften the stiffening agent in the canvas. Gently pull the canvas into shape.

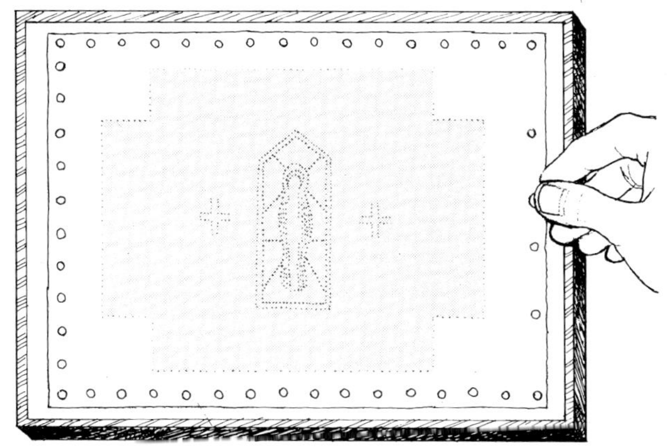

Cover the board with blotting paper and lay embroidery face down. Pin, and working from center out, stretch the canvas evenly. Align threads with straight edge of board.

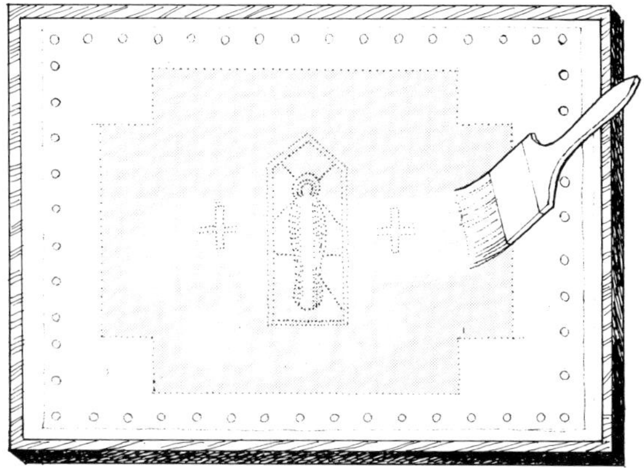

Brush the back of the embroidery only with a coating of strong wallpaper paste. This will hold the shape and protect the embroidery. Leave to dry thoroughly.

Covering the pad with calico

For best results, the foam pad should be well-compressed and wrapped firmly in calico before inserting into the kneeler. Cut sufficient calico to wrap the foam like a parcel, about 30 in x 32 in for a 10 in x 15 in x 3 in kneeler. Pull the fabric firmly, pin and hem the folds in place.

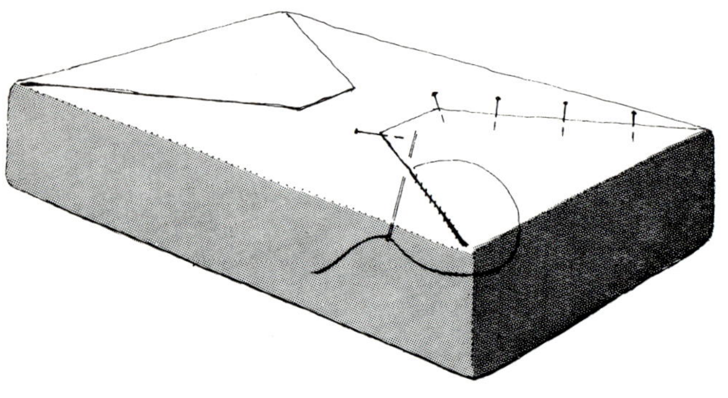

Mitering a corner

This is the simplest and most effective way to neaten corners which are to be faced, especially on heavy fabrics where it is essential to reduce bulky turnings.

Cut corner diagonally across trimming fabric to within $\frac{1}{2}$ in of worked area (A). Fold the $\frac{1}{2}$ in turning to the back of the work and press. Then fold the turnings so that the two edges meet (B). Hold in place with herringbone stitch (C).

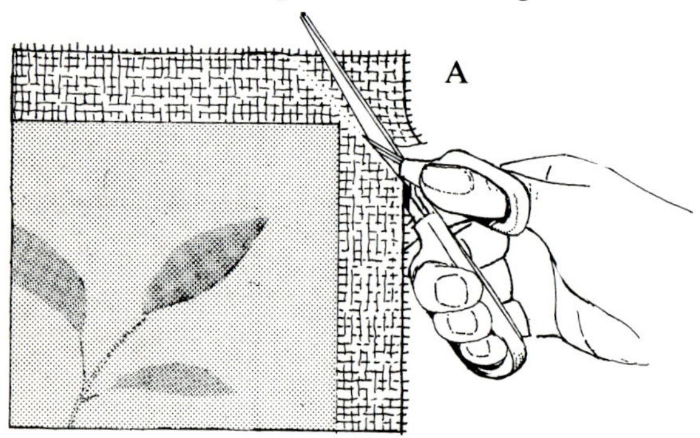

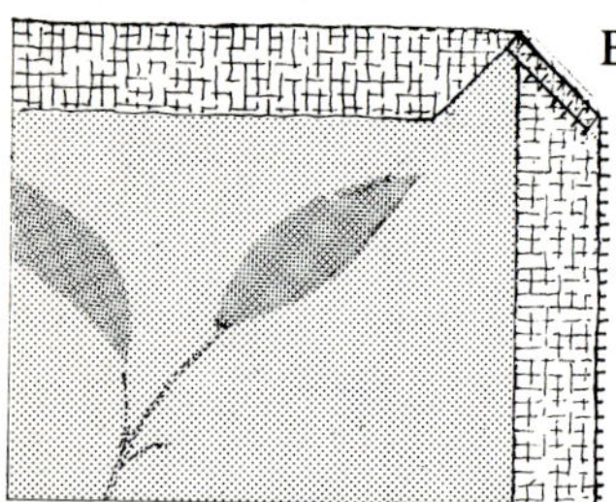

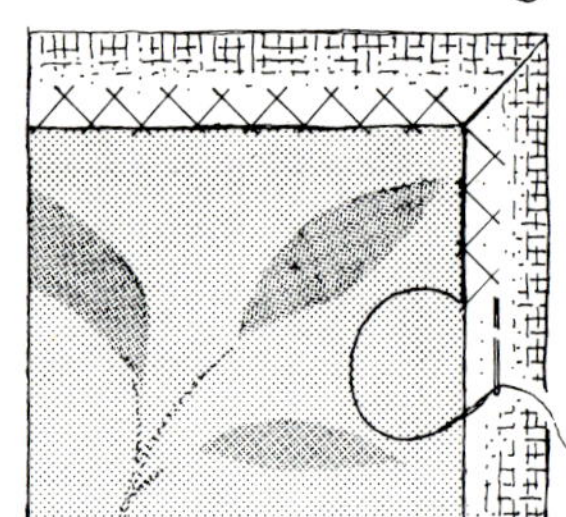

Lacing the back of the kneeler

To form a good rectangular shape using firm fabrics, it is advisable to lace the back of the kneeler with strong linen thread. Work from the center out pulling the canvas evenly.

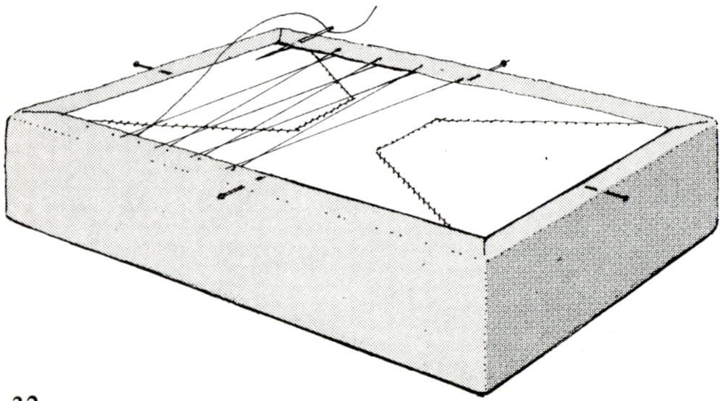

Mounting fabric on card

Cut fabric to required size adding extra 1 in turnings all round. Mark center of card and edges of fabric both ways. Place card on wrong side of fabric, match register marks and pin firmly into edges of card. Miter corners and using strong thread, lace across working outwards from the middle (A). Repeat lacing in the opposite direction, pulling fabric gently and evenly (B).

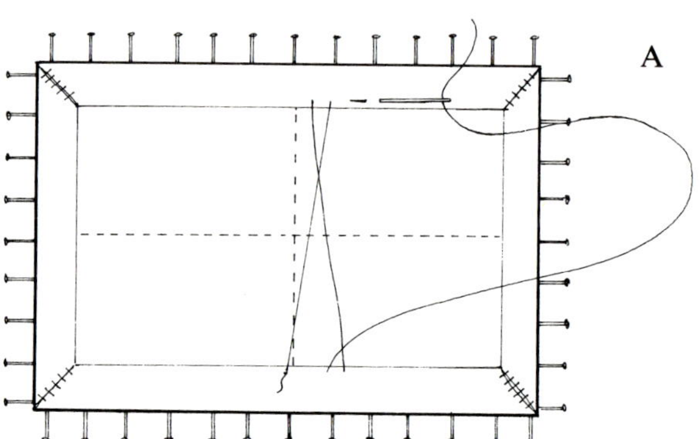

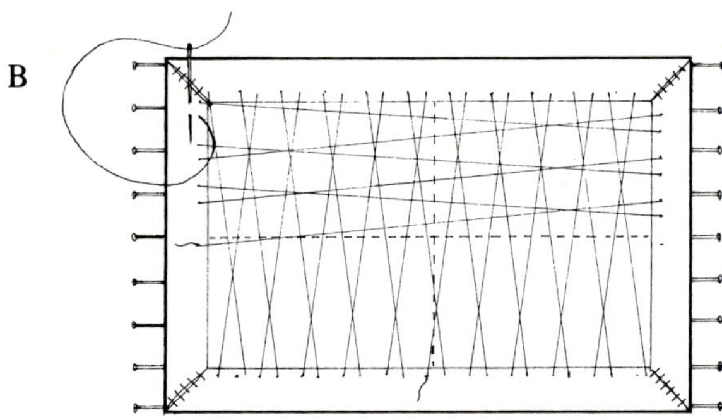

Stitching the spine to the burse

Fold turnings on spine lining so that it measures $\frac{3}{4}$ in x width of fronts. With wrong sides outside, pin over top edges of lining boards. Neatly overcast both sides with matching thread (A). The burse spine and fronts are glued in place and the top edges invisibly stitched with matching thread (B).

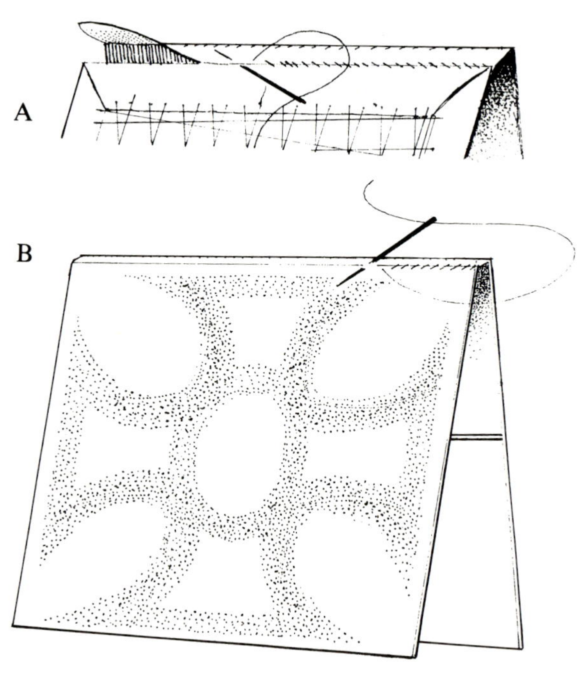